FOOD
for the
CITY

D1293116

FOOD
—— for the ——
CITY

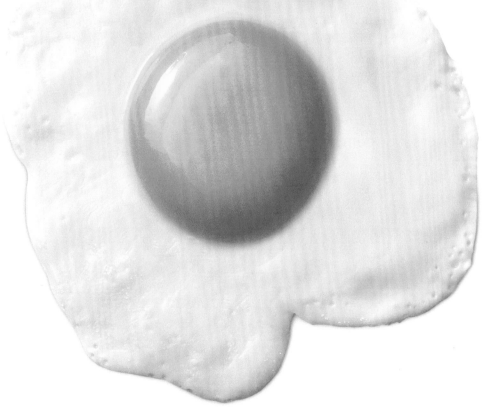

A Future for the Metropolis

NAi Publishers / Stroom Den Haag

FOOD
for the
CITY

Contents

Foreword: Nancy Walsh Saves the World

Arno van Roosmalen
Director of Stroom Den Haag

Can art solve the world's problems? You might think so, reading the title of a sprawling, magnificent floor sculpture by the American artist Walter de Maria: *A Computer Which Will Solve Every Problem in the World / 3 – 12 Polygon*. Yet this work of art was not the centrepiece of the World Economic Forum in Davos, nor did European leaders hold a special summit in Museum Boijmans van Beuningen, which has it in its collection.

In a corner of the exhibition *Living Remains* by the Mexican artist Raul Ortega Ayala at Stroom Den Haag the installation *Nancy Walsh – Cheese Made of Mother's Milk* was on display. On a small table with a subdued white table-cloth stood a plate with a few crackers and a dish of cream-coloured cheese, with a notice next to it inviting visitors to have a taste. It was as if there were a circle drawn on the floor – invisible, but inviolable. Only a handful of visitors dared to transgress this boundary.

The requirements of hygiene had been met; Nancy Walsh had given her consent; the whole thing was perfectly legal. And yet . . . visitors declined to participate, saying, 'It feels a little like cannibalism', 'Isn't this intended for a defenceless baby?' and 'It's much too intimate for me'. The power of Ortega Ayala's work is that he coaxes people into taking a personal stand. They feel empathy, shame, disgust, incredulity, scepticism, or pity – powerful emotions – but they take a moral decision.

Paragraph 25 of the Universal Declaration of Human Rights (1948) states that 'everyone has the right to a standard of living adequate for the health and well-being of himself and of his family, including food . . .' The global food situation is so precarious that in reality many of the world's citizens seem to be denied their right to food. This is true now and will certainly be true in the future. Climate change, continental water management, geopolitics, and food speculation are enormous problems. People are searching for solutions through governance, by legal means, and with the aid of science and politics.

In her Cleveringa Lecture (2005), the Dutch scientist Louise Fresco points out that in the three monotheistic religions, the very earliest law relates to food, specifically to eating a forbidden fruit. Food stands at the beginning of all moral awareness. Food implies many dangers: not only health risks, but also challenges to values and ways of life. This is why a religious authority was needed to determine what was safe to eat. Fresco concludes that we need a new paradigm, 'a coherent set of rules of conduct for individuals, government bodies, businesses, and civil society, so that food can once again become central to a fair and sustainable global society' – in other words, new dietary laws.

Laws are more than technical decrees and go deeper than a formalized social contract. You can force people to obey laws by disseminating information about them and establishing an authority to enforce them. You can also coax people into complying with laws. In that case, it is essential that there be a mutual understanding of the importance of the law and a degree of engagement that includes internalization of the deeper significance of the law.

Art can play a role in this process through its capacity to create unprecedented situations, present parallel worlds, and make the invisible visible. In these ways, art can spark individual awareness of ethical, social, or political issues and speak to the motivations, convictions, or emotions underlying rules or laws. One of the causes of the food crisis is the growing consumption of meat. The UN could instate an annual meat ration; art offers a different approach. For years, the British artist John O'Shea has been working on projects that examine the ethics of eating meat. This theme is most explicit in *The Meat Licence Proposal*, in which O'Shea proposes a new law: you cannot receive a licence to buy meat until you have slaughtered an animal yourself. The project documents his legal battle but also reveals the discrepancy between the affection that people feel for animals and the institutionalized nature of animal slaughter. By challenging our unquestioned assumptions about eating meat, O'Shea plants the seed of an ethically, legally, and perhaps, in the long run, politically grounded set of rules – a system of dietary law for a better world, based on experience.

While, unfortunately, there is no computer that can solve all our problems, there is an inspiring and influential source of critical awareness – namely, art. Art therefore deserves a place at the heart of our society. Isn't it fantastic that while this publication is the initiative of an arts organization, Stroom Den Haag, it brings together visionary writings by authors with diverse social and cultural backgrounds, writings that can inspire reflection and action?

Timeline

Before Common Era

2050 BCE

Legal Jargon: The stone cuneiform tablet of Ur-Nammu is the oldest remaining law document, and introduced the 'if-then' argument into legal writing, a form of argument still commonly used today. Furthermore, it allowed for judicial decisions, and damages to be paid for actions. Other government records that the Sumerians created around this time include records of the distribution of barley rations to the workmen and their families at the Temple of Bau. The text dictates that adults received around 40 sila, or pints, per month and children received 20. From the prologue of Ur-Nammu's tablet, this passage invokes deities and decrees equality:

'...After An and Enlil had turned over the Kingship of Ur to Nanna, at that time did Ur-Nammu, son born of Ninsun, for his beloved mother who bore him, in accordance with his principles of equity and truth... Then did Ur-Nammu the mighty warrior, king of Ur, king of Sumer and Akkad, by the might of Nanna, lord of the city, and in accordance with the true word of Utu, establish equity in the land; he banished malediction, violence and strife, and set the monthly Temple expenses at 90 gur of barley, 30 sheep, and 30 sila of butter. He fashioned the bronze sila-measure, standardized the one-mina weight, and standardized the stone weight of a shekel of silver in relation to one mina.... The orphan was not delivered up to the rich man; the widow was not delivered up to the mighty man; the man of one shekel was not delivered up to the man of one mina.'

1312 BCE

Kosher: The Torah (part of the Tanakh) are the founding religious documents of the Jewish religion, and its founding legal and ethical texts. In the Torah there is much discussion about what is permissible to eat, both religiously and ethically. These laws are called kashrut; foods in accord with the laws are called kosher. Such laws include not eating animals that don't chew cud, not mixing milk and meat, but permit eating water creatures with fins and scales; on the list of appropriate foods are insects such as grasshoppers and locusts.

Deuteronomy 14:6 'You may eat any animal that has a divided hoof and that chews the cud.'

Leviticus 11:9 'These shall ye eat of all that are in the waters: whatsoever hath fins and scales in the waters, in the seas, and in the rivers, them shall ye eat. And all that have not fins and scales in the seas, and in the rivers, of all that move in the waters, and of any living thing which is in the waters, they shall be an abomination unto you: They shall be even an abomination unto you: ye shall not eat of their flesh, but ye shall have their carcasses in abomination.

whatsoever hath no fins nor scales in the waters, that shall be an abomination unto you.

Leviticus 11:22 'Of these you may eat any kind of locust, katydid, cricket or grasshopper.'

Deuteronomy 14:21 'Do not eat anything you find already dead. You may give it to the foreigner residing in any of your towns, and they may eat it, or you may sell it to any other foreigner. But you are a people holy to the LORD your God. Do not cook a young goat in its mother's milk.'

Leviticus 7:26-27 'And wherever you live, you must not eat the blood of any bird or animal. Anyone who eats blood must be cut off from their people.'

Genesis 1:29-30 'Then God said, "Behold, I have given you every plant yielding seed that is on the [a] surface of all the earth, and every tree [b] which has fruit yielding seed; it shall be food for you; and to every beast of the earth and to every bird of the [a]sky and to every thing that[b]moves on the earth [c] which has life, I have given every green plant for food"; and it was so.'

Pythagoras in Ovid, The Metamorphoses:

'Alas, what wickedness to swallow flesh into our own flesh, to fatten our greedy bodies by cramming in other bodies, to have one living creature fed by the death of another! In the midst of such wealth as earth, the best of mothers, provides, nothing forsooth satisfies you, but to behave like the Cyclopes, inflicting sorry wounds with cruel teeth! You cannot appease the hungry cravings of your wicked, gluttonous stomachs except by destroying some other life.'

580–500 BCE

Five Contemplations: Siddhārtha Gautama was a spiritual teacher from the north-eastern Indian subcontinent, regarded as the supreme Buddha, which means the enlightened (or awakened) one. Buddhists believe that if food is chosen carefully, it will correspond with the amount of light entering in the body, which affects their inner power necessary to climb the spiritual ladder. A Buddhist is required to contemplate these five things when eating:

1 I think about where the food came from and the amount of work necessary to grow the food, transport it, prepare and cook it and bring it to the table.

2 I contemplate my own virtuous nature. Is it sufficient to merit receiving the food as offering?

3 I guard my mind against transgression, the principal ones being greed and so forth.

4 I realize that food is a wholesome medicine that heals the sufferings of the body.

5 I should receive the food offerings only for the sake of realizing the Way.

563–483 BCE

Iron Ploughs: The plough was invented by the Chinese and consisted of a wooden frame and a cast iron share. It was later heavily promoted and popularized during the Han Dynasty. The advanced design had a sharp point for cutting soil and wings that moved the soil out of the way and reduced friction. Horses were introduced around the 1st century BCE, but still the technology was not introduced in England or Holland until the 17th century.

475–221 BCE

250 BCE–200 CE

Bhagavad-Gita: There is much discussion about when the Bhagavad-Gita, or the main Hindu Sanskrit texts, were written. Some scholars place them between the 5th and 2nd century BCE, while others claim they are from the Common Era. Regardless, as with many religious texts, there were passages that laid out dietary law. **From Bhagavad-Gita 9:27:**

> 'If one offers Me with love and devotion a leaf, a flower, fruit or water, I will accept it.' Many assumed that Lord Krishna (the narrator in this scripture) is entreating that no meat, fish, or eggs should be offered or eaten, and to this day many Hindus maintain a vegetarian diet. Further, according to Vedic (Hindu scripture) texts, one should offer all food as a sacrifice to God: '...all that you do, all that you eat, all that you offer and give away, as well as all austerities that you may perform, should be done as an offering unto Me.'

240 BCE

Row Planting: Master Lu wrote in the *Spring and Autumn Annals:*

> 'If the crops are grown in rows they will mature rapidly because they will not interfere with each other's growth. The horizontal rows must be well drawn, the vertical rows made with skill, for if the lines are straight the wind will pass gently through.'

This technique of planting in rows allows for crops to grow faster and stronger, and makes for easier planting, maintenance, and harvesting. It is used widely today.

160 BCE

On Running a Farm: Roman-born Marcus Cato penned *De Agri Cultura*, a manual on running a farm (and, as it turns out, on running a wife), that contains a variety of rules of husbandry and management, including proper equipment for oil and wine cellars. It was used as a textbook for Romans during a period of agricultural expansion, and assumes the farm will be staffed and run by slaves. Cato even advises keeping slaves working nonstop, reducing rations when they are sick, and selling slaves when they are past their prime.

> 'It is true that to obtain money by trade is sometimes more profitable, were it not so hazardous; and likewise money-lending, if it were as honourable. Our ancestors held this view and embodied it in their laws, which required that the thief be mulcted double and the usurer fourfold; how much less desirable a citizen they considered the usurer than the thief, one may judge from this.'
>
> 'And when they would praise a worthy man their praise took this form: 'good husbandman, good farmer'; one so praised was thought to have received the greatest commendation.'
>
> 'The trader I consider to be an energetic man, and one bent on making money; but, as I said above, it is a dangerous career and one subject to disaster.'
>
> 'On the other hand, it is from the farming class that the bravest men and the sturdiest soldiers come, their calling is most highly respected, their livelihood is most assured and is looked on with the least hostility, and those who are engaged in that pursuit are least inclined to be disaffected. And now, to come back to my subject, the above will

serve as an introduction to what I have undertaken.

'See that the housekeeper performs all her duties. If the master has given her to you as wife, keep yourself only to her. Make her stand in awe of you. Restrain her from extravagance. She must visit the neighbouring and other women very seldom, and not have them either in the house or in her part of it. She must not go out to meals, or be a gadabout. She must not engage in religious worship herself or get others to engage in it for her without the orders of the master or the mistress; let her remember that the master attends to the devotions for the whole household. She must be neat herself, and keep the farmstead neat and clean. She must clean and tidy the hearth every night before she goes to bed.'

'Land ought to be drained during the winter, and the drain-ditches on the hillsides kept clean. The greatest danger from water is in the early autumn, when there is dust. When the rains begin, the whole household must turn out with shovels and hoes, open the ditches, turn the water into the roads, and see that it flows off. You should look around the farmstead while it is raining, and mark all leaks with charcoal, so that the tile can be replaced after the rain stops. During the growing season, if water is standing anywhere, in the grain or the seed-bed or in ditches, or if there is any obstruction to the water, it should be cleared, opened and removed.'

Common Era

650 CE

Halal: Passages from the Qur'an informed Islamic jurisprudence on many laws, including dietary. This holy book of Islam expounds on what the Prophet Mohammed said and did, such as being forbidden to eat swine, drink alcohol, or use animals which have died on their own. The foods that are permitted are called Halal, a term commonly used today in both Islamic and non-Islamic countries.

'He has only forbidden to you dead animals, blood, the flesh of swine, and that which has been dedicated to other than Allah. But whoever is forced [by necessity], neither desiring [it] nor transgressing [its limit], there is no sin upon him. Indeed, Allah is Forgiving and Merciful.'

Surat Al-Baqarah, 2:173

650 CE

Ramadhan:

'The month of Ramadhan [is that] in which was revealed the Qur'an, a guidance for the people and clear proofs of guidance and criterion. So whoever sights [the new moon of] the month, let him fast it; and whoever is ill or on a journey - then an equal number of other days. Allah intends for you ease and does not intend for you hardship and [wants] for you to complete the period and to glorify Allah for that [to] which He has guided you; and perhaps you will be grateful.'

1257 CE

Capitalist Agriculture: In Bologna, Italy, 6000 serfs, or agricultural labourers, were freed in exchange for the receipt of half their produce. This was considered a move toward the first capitalist system of agriculture.

1475 CE

Liber de Arte Coquinaria: The *Liber de Arte Coquinaria, or The Art of Cooking*, is the first known culinary guide to specify ingredients, cooking times, and techniques, utensils, and amounts. Written by Maestro Martino, the book also details a significant shift from Medieval to Renaissance cooking and conviviality.

1516 CE

Utopia: Sir Thomas More's novel *Utopia* provides social commentary of the evils of contemporary society. In his Utopia, city-dwellers are sent to the countryside to work so that they can stay connected to agriculture.

'They have built farmhouses over the whole country, which are well contrived and furnished with all things necessary for country labour. Inhabitants for them are sent in rotation from the cities. No family in the country hath fewer than forty men and women in it, beside two slaves. A master and mistress preside over every family, and over thirty families a magistrate. Every year twenty of the family return to town after having been two years in the country, and in their place other twenty are sent to learn country business of those who have been there only one year, and must, in their turn, teach the next comers. Thus, those who live on the farms are never ignorant of agriculture, and commit no fatal errors, such as causing a scarcity of corn.'

1566 CE

Seed Drill: The seed drill was used by the Chinese during the Han Dynasty, but first patented to Camillot Torello by the Venetian Senate during the 16th Century. It is used to plant seeds into the soil at a uniform depth, and cover them. The previous method of tossing seeds by hand was wasteful and inefficient, causing uneven growth; this allowed for neat rows and more efficient crop management.

1742 CE

Faneuil Hall: Created as a meeting place and market in Boston, Massachusetts, Faneuil Hall was created to foster urban renewal with food as an attraction. It housed merchants, fishmongers, butchers, and produce sellers, while providing a place for soapbox speeches by famous orators. In 1764, colonists used this space to protest against the Sugar Act and established the creed 'no taxation without representation'. Today it still holds restaurants and markets, as well as theatres and other shops.

1803 CE

Restaurant Guide: Alexandre Balthazar Laurent Grimod de La Reynière, a Parisian lawyer, creates the first restaurant guide after wandering through Paris and noting all the restaurants and what they serve. This provided practical information, but also set critical standards paving the way for the juxtaposition of critic and restaurant guide. The trend of giving great dinner parties began to give way to clamouring for the latest and greatest new restaurant.

1809 CE

Canning: French Emperor Napoleon Bonaparte, who has been credited with saying 'an army marches of its stomach', issued a contest and reward for the first person to come up with a portable food preservation method for his army on its long marches. It took almost 15 years, but finally Nicolas Appert, a French confectioner and chef, created a system similar to how wine was being preserved, in airtight glass bottles. He was awarded 12,000 francs for his efforts. Soon after, techniques for canning in metal tins were developed.

1815–1846 CE

Corn Laws: The British Corn Laws were a series of statutes enacted between 1815 and 1846 that kept corn prices at a high level. This measure was intended to protect English farmers from cheap foreign imports of grain following the end of the Napoleonic Wars. In 1846 the government under Sir Robert Peel was persuaded to repeal the Corn Laws.

1820–1835 CE

Railway: Modern rail transport systems were first appearing in England and mainland Europe in the 1820s, the most notable being the Great Western railway. This opened up routes to bring food into cities from the agricultural hinterlands.

1840 CE

Fertilizer: German chemist Justus von Leibig proclaimed in *Die organische Chemie in ihrer Anwendung auf Agricultur und Physiologie* (Chemistry in Its Applications to Agriculture and Physiology) that because 'perfect agriculture is the true foundation of all trade and industry', a 'rational system of agriculture cannot be formed without the application of scientific principles'. Though his own attempts at altering the soil with chemical manures weren't effective, his work ultimately led to the discovery of superphosphates, which were developed into fertilizers.

1844 CE

Cooperative: Though there were earlier cooperatives, it was the Rochdale Society of Equitable Pioneers in the UK that became the prototype for future consumer cooperatives with principles like the 'one member, one vote' system and open membership.

1854 CE

Walden: In his book *Walden* Henry David Thoreau wrote 'Our life is frittered away by detail. An honest man has hardly need to count more than his ten fingers, or in extreme cases he may add his ten toes, and lump the rest. Simplicity, simplicity, simplicity!' about getting back to nature, ridding oneself of material possessions, and other romanticized ideas of self-reliance and living off the land.

1862 CE

Pasteurization: In studying germ theory, the French scientist Louis Pasteur showed that the growth of micro-organisms was related to bad drinks, such as milk that has gone off. With colleague Claude Bernard he established and tested a process to kill the bacteria and mould by heating liquids to specified temperatures. This process became known as pasteurization.

1862 CE

Homestead Act: In the United States, this law provided opportunity for anyone who had never taken up arms against the government, including freed slaves, to file an application to claim federal land. The area would be called a homestead, and required three steps: application, improvement on land, and filing for a deed. Homesteads were typically areas west of the Mississippi River and consisted of about 65 hectares. The act displaced many Native Americans, and officially ended in 1976.

1894 CE

Marx on Agriculture: German philosopher and renowned socialist Karl Marx wrote in *Das Kapital:* 'The moral of the tale (...) is that the capitalist system runs counter to a rational agriculture, or that a rational agriculture is incompatible with the capitalist system (even if the latter promotes technical development in agriculture) and needs either small farmers working for themselves or the control of the associated producers.'

1898 CE

Garden City: The Garden City movement was initiated by Sir Ebenezer Howard in his book *To-Morrow: a Peaceful Path to Real Reform*, with the intention of sparking planned and self-contained communities surrounded by parks and green spaces. Each area would be split between industry, housing and farmlands. The ideal 'garden city' would be about 2,400 hectares formed in concentric patterns with a full population of around 32,000. Garden cities would be linked by rail to form networks.

1900 CE

Michelin Guide: Andre Michelin published the first edition of the guide in 1900 to help drivers maintain their cars, find decent lodging, and eat well while touring France. It included addresses of filling stations, mechanics, and tire dealers, along with local prices for fuel, tires, and auto repairs. Today, top restaurants all over the world seek a Michelin star or three.

1906 CE

The Jungle: Journalist Upton Sinclair penned this novel after going undercover in Chicago meatpacking plants to illuminate the plight of an immigrant in the United States. Instead of focusing on the plight of the Lithuanian main character, readers were alarmed by the detailed description of corruption in the plants. Sinclair was quoted saying: 'I aimed at the public's heart, and by accident I hit it in the stomach.' Pressure from the public led to the Meat Inspection Act, and the Pure Food and Drug Act of 1906. This established what would later become the Food and Drug Administration. From *The Jungle*:

'This is no fairy story and no joke; [T]he meat would be shoveled into carts, and the man who did the shoveling would not trouble to lift out a rat even when he saw one – there were things that went into the sausage in comparison with which a poisoned rat was a tidbit. There was no place for the men to wash their hands before they ate their dinner, and so they made a practice of washing them in the water that was to be ladled into the sausage. There were the butt-ends of smoked meat, and the scraps of corned beef, and all the odds and ends of the waste of the plants, that would be dumped into old barrels in the cellar and left there. Under the system of rigid economy which the packers enforced, there were some jobs that it only paid to do once in a long time, and among these was the cleaning out of the waste barrels. Every spring they did it; and in the barrels would be dirt and rust and old nails and stale water – and cartload after cartload of it would be taken up and dumped into the hoppers with fresh meat, and sent out to the public's breakfast.

1912 CE

Automated Servers: In the Edgar Rice Burrows book *A Princess of Mars*, the author imagines restaurants were food is served by automated mechanical serving apparatus.

'Kantos Kan led me to one of these gorgeous eating places where we were served entirely by mechanical apparatus. No hand touched the food from the time it entered the building in its raw state until it emerged hot and delicious upon the tables before the guests, in response to the touching of tiny buttons to indicate their desires.'

1916 CE

Grocery Store: The Piggly Wiggly was the world's first supermarket, opened in Memphis, Tennessee by Clarence Saunders. Before, shoppers had come to markets with a written order, to be filled by clerks; Saunders believed that a new method was needed to save time and expense, thus the self-service market was born. New features included checkout stands, individually priced products, and refrigerated cases for longer storage time. It is now the standard in many countries.

1917 CE

Victory Garden: British and American citizens were encouraged to cultivate fruits and vegetables during WWI on private and public lands that were empty or otherwise available. The gardens were meant to reduce the pressure of public demand during the war years when foods were rationed and scarcer and were needed to feed the troops. The gardens gained many fans, including First Lady Eleanor Roosevelt who planted on the White House lawn and encouraged their revival during WWII.

1921 CE

White Castle: Founded in Wichita, Kansas, this fast food joint was created to look sterile and clean – white porcelain and steel – measures meant to counter the public suspicion of beef following the release of *The Jungle*. Owner Walter A. Anderson is credited with standardizing the production and serving of food, as well as the invention of the hamburger bun. Americans eat between one to three hamburgers per week on average.

1923 CE

Hybrid Corn: The first commercial hybrid, called Copper Cross, was produced in 1923. Though toyed with since before the turn of the century, hybrid corn became a hit during the 1930s as the Depression hit the US, becoming the first successful product combining two pure strains. The hybrids proved more vigorous, withstanding harsh weather and deflecting diseases and pests better than non-hybrid brands. Farmers were able to produce more corn per acre with these vigorous hybrids. Within 20 years, 90 per cent of the corn grown was hybrid corn.

1929–1940 CE

Kolkhoz: Stalin enforced collectivization with the objective of consolidating land and labour, creating collective farms called *kolkhozes*. Stalin believed that by replacing peasant farms with these collective farms the food supply would increase substantially and gain the Soviet Union greater exports. This would be the solution to the agricultural distribution crisis. Collective farms had existed peacefully before the Stalin enforcement, but with the forced collectivization, things quickly became bloody. The *kolkhoz* did not live up to the expectations of production.

1932 CE

Broadacre City: American Architect Frank Lloyd Wright first proposed Broadacre City in his book *The Disappearing City*, but it was an idea he stuck with through much of his life. Created as the opposite of the city as it was, as a divine idea of a new suburbia, giving each family one acre of land from federal reserves. With the land spread the way it was, it was estimated that there would be 500 people per square mile, which is lower than current densities (often two or three thousand per square mile). In *The Disappearing City* Wright presented Broadacre City:

'The broad acre city, where every family will have at least an acre of land, is the inevitable municipality of the future (...) We live now in cities of the past, slaves of the machine and of traditional building. We cannot solve our living and transportation problems by burrowing under or climbing over, and why should we? We will spread out, and in so doing will transform our human habitation sites into those allowing beauty of design and landscaping, sanitation and fresh air, privacy and playgrounds, and a plot whereon to raise things.'

1934 CE

Synthetic Food: In the book *Twilight* John W. Campbell (under the pseudonym Don A. Stuart) wrote about a machine that could make any food from the basic elements, without the need of agriculture:

'The restaurant had the food displayed directly, and I made a choice. The food was three hundred thousand years old, I suppose. I didn't know, and the machines that served it to me didn't care, for they made things synthetically, you see, and perfectly.'

1944 CE

Ready Meals: In 1944, frozen dinners were being served on airplanes; by 1954, Swanson's first TV Dinners were introduced to fulfil two post-war trends: timesaving modern appliances and the growing fascination with television. More than 10 million TV dinners were sold during the Swanson's first year of national distribution.

1945 CE

FAO: FAO, or the Food and Agriculture Organization, is a specialized agency of the United Nations that works on efforts to defeat hunger. The FAO acts as a neutral forum where developed and developing countries can meet as equals to negotiate agreements and policy. In 2000, the FAO created the Millennium Development Goals in tandem with the United Nations Millennium Declaration; the goals state the following:

Goal 2: Achieve universal primary education

Goal 3: Promote gender equality and empower women

Goal 4: Reduce child mortality

Goal 5: Improve maternal health

Goal 6: Combat HIV/AIDS, malaria and other diseases

Goal 7: Ensure environmental sustainability

Goal 8: Develop a Global Partnership for Development

Critics say that the goals were plagued with a lack of evidence-based theory to justify choosing these objectives, and also a lack of focus on local participation and empowerment. Also, the goals as they are do not define a road map to achievement.

1947 CE

Agriculture Act of 1947: **After German U-boats cut off supplies to Britain, the Agriculture Act was created and promoted a slash, dump, and spray approach to farming in the name of productivity. This was the beginning of factory farming practices in Britain, as the bill also granted subsidies to farmers to encourage greater output by introducing new technology, specialization and improved breeding and management of animals. From the act:**

'The following provisions of this Part of this Act shall have effect for the purpose of promoting and maintaining, by the provision of guaranteed prices and assured markets for the produce mentioned in the First Schedule to this Act, a stable and efficient agricultural industry capable of producing such part of the nation's food and other agricultural produce as in the national interest it is desirable to produce in the United Kingdom, and of producing it at minimum prices consistently with proper remuneration and living conditions for farmers and workers in agriculture and an adequate return on capital invested in the industry.'

1948 CE

World Health Organisation: **The World Health Organization (WHO) is a specialized agency of the United Nations (UN) established in Geneva, Switzerland. The WHO acts as an authority on issues concerning global public health, including the outbreak of diseases and the promotion of prevention.**

1951 CE

Planet for Food Production: **Famed science fiction writer Isaac Asimov re-imagined the world when its limits had been tested; food needed to be imported, not just from another country, but from another planet. In *Foundation Series*, Asimov wrote:**

'Its urbanization, progressing steadily, had finally reached the ultimate. All the land surface of Trantor, 75,000,000 square miles in extent, was a single city. The population, at its height, was well in excess of forty billions. This enormous population was devoted almost entirely to the administrative necessities of Empire, and found themselves all too few for the complications of the task. (It is to be remembered that the impossibility of proper administration of the Galactic Empire under the uninspired leadership of the later Emperors was a considerable factor in the Fall.) Daily, fleets of ships in the tens of thousands brought the produce of twenty agricultural worlds to the dinner tables of Trantor . . .'

'Its dependence upon the outer worlds for food and, indeed, for all necessities of life, made Trantor increasingly vulnerable to conquest by siege. In the last millennium of the Empire, the monotonously numerous revolts made Emperor after Emperor conscious of this, and Imperial policy became little more than the protection of Trantor's delicate jugular vein . . .'

1952 CE

Meat in a Vat: **The theme of meat or other food grown in a vat to alleviate the pressures of growing populations was repeated in several science fiction novels. In the quote below, Frederik Pohl writes about Chicken Little, in which tissue-cultured meat is grown as a food source. Frank Herbert explored lab-grown meat in *Whipping Star* in 1969, and William Gibson also explores the topic in his book *Neuromancer* in 1984. Frederik Pohl (w/C.M. Kornbluth) wrote about it in *The Space Merchants*:**

'Scum-skimming wasn't hard to learn. You got up at dawn. You gulped a breakfast sliced not long ago from Chicken Little and washed it down with Coffiest. You put on your coveralls and took the cargo net up to your tier. In blazing noon from sunrise to sunset you walked your acres of shallow tanks crusted with algae. If you walked slowly, every thirty seconds or so you spotted a patch at maturity, bursting with yummy carbohydrates. You skimmed the patch with your skimmer and slung it down the well, where it would be baled, or processed into glucose to feed Chicken Little, who would be sliced and packed to feed people from Baffinland to Little America.'

1955 CE

Algae as Food: **Philip K. Dick first wrote about using algae as a food source in *Solar Lottery*, a theme that was repeated two years later in *Cities in Flight* by James Blish. Here, Dick describes the process by which it is made, from *Solar Lottery*:**

'Ted Benteley stood by the kitchen door inhaling warm smells of cooking food. The Davis house was pleasant and bright. Al Davis, minus his shoes, was sitting contentedly before the tv set in the living room, gazing earnestly at the ads. His pretty brown-haired wife Laura was preparing dinner.

"If that's protine," Benteley said to her, "It's the best job of adulteration I've ever smelled."

"We never have protine," Laura answered briskly. "We tried it the first year we were married, but you can taste it no matter how they fix it up. It's terribly costly to buy natural foods, of course, but it's worth it."

"Protine isn't a natural algae. It's a mutant that started out in culture tanks in the Middle East and gradually crept onto a variety of fresh-water surfaces."

"It also grows over the Great Lakes . . . "'

Southdale Shopping Centre · Located in Edina, Minnesota, this is the oldest fully enclosed

European feeling of a meeting place that many American cities lacked.

1961 CE

Butcher Plant:
This science fiction novel by Clifford Simak talks about a meat-bearing plant that can be grown like any other vegetable. Author H. Beam Piper wrote about a similar idea in his book *Four-Day Planet*. Simak described it in *Time is the Simplest Thing*:

'They're taking away our very livelihood. They're destroying a fine system of conventions and of ethics built very painfully through the centuries by men deeply dedicated to the public service (...) There is the matter for example, of this so-called butcher vegetable. You plant a row of seeds, then later you go out and dig up the plants as you would potatoes, but rather than potatoes you have hunks of protein.'

'And so,' said Blaine, 'for the first time in their lives, millions of people are eating meat they couldn't buy before, that your fine, brave system of conventions and of ethics didn't allow them to earn enough to buy.'

'But the farmers!' Dalton yelled. 'And the meat market operators. Not to mention the packing interests . . .'

'I suppose,' suggested Blaine, 'it would've been more cricket if the seeds had been sold exclusively to the farmers or the supermarkets. Or if they were sold at the rate of a dollar or a dollar and a half a piece instead of 10 cents a packet . . .'

1961 CE

World Food Programme:
Though established in 1961, this organization was not meant to be running until 1963. But when in 1962 an earthquake shook Iran, a hurricane blew through Thailand, and Algeria established independence (which led to a flood of returning refugees), the World Food Programme came into action when food assistance was urgent, opening its doors early to address the hunger issues worldwide. Since its inception, WFP has provided food for more than 1.4 billion people, investing over $30 billion (USD) in emergency relief and development.

1961 CE

Codex Alimentarius:
Between 1897 and 1911, the Austro-Hungarian Empire developed a collection of standards and product descriptions for a wide variety of foods called the *Codex Alimentarius Austriacus*. It lacked legality, but was used as a reference by the courts. Present-day Codex Alimentarius was developed in 1961 by the joint task of FAO/WHO to protect public health and fair practices in the food industry, and has become a global reference for food industry regulations in developed and developing countries. The Codex Alimentarius officially covers all foods, whether processed, semi-processed or raw, but the most attention has been given to foods that are marketed directly to consumers. It's available in Arabic, Chinese, English, French and Spanish, making it easier for developing countries throughout Africa and Asia to respond to and introduce food legislation and/or by establishing or strengthening food control agencies to monitor compliance with such regulations.

1962 CE

Silent Spring:
Rachel Carson wrote this book, which documented the detrimental effects of pesticides on the environment, particularly on birds. Carson accused the chemical industry of spreading disinformation, and public officials of accepting industry claims uncritically. After release of the book, restrictions were placed on the pesticide DDT. Carson, with the book as her vehicle, is widely credited with launching the Environmental Movement. Critics claim a rise in malaria since. Monsanto, the seed company, published a response later that year called *The Desolate Year* touting the need for pesticides. Carson wrote:

'The earth's vegetation is part of a web of life in which there are intimate and essential relations between plants and animals. Sometimes we have no choice but to disturb these relationships, but we should do so thoughtfully, with full awareness that what we do may have consequences remote in time and place.'

'It is not possible to add pesticides to water anywhere without threatening the purity of water everywhere.

Seldom if ever does Nature operate in closed and separate compartments, and she has not done so in distributing the earth's water supply.'

Monsanto's response in *The Desolate Year* (1962):

'For, without pesticides, the pest control firms had automatically gone out of business. Of a sudden, some of the starkness of the times dawned on other people. No more protection against moths in clothing, furniture, carpets; no weapons except a fly swatter against rampant bedbugs, silverfish, fleas, slithering cockroaches, and spreading ants. More people shuddered, then, and still the desolate year was young.'

1965 CE

Poison Snooper:
In the world of *Dune*, a science fiction novel created by Frank Herbert, the affluent – especially the noble – needed to be careful about poisons in their food and drink, and so used a poison snooper for detection.

'The Duke said: "Paul, I'm doing a hateful thing, but I must." He stood beside the portable poison snooper that had been brought into the conference room for their breakfast. The thing's sensor arms hung limply over the table, reminding Paul of some weird insect newly dead. The Duke's attention was directed out the windows at the landing field and its roiling of dust against the morning sky.'

1966–1976 CE

Cultural Revolution:
During Mao Zedong's Cultural Revolution in China, privileged urban youth and certain intellectuals would be sent to mountainous and farming villages to learn from the farmers and workers. This policy, named Down to the Countryside Movement, was a result of the anti-bourgeois thinking that would displace many during this period. Historian Mobo Gao wrote in his essay book *The Battle for China's Past:*

'The Cultural Revolution involved many millions of people who willingly participated in what they saw as a movement to better Chinese society and humanity in general. A whole range of ideas and issues from politics to education and healthcare, from incubators and the arts to industrial and agricultural policies were examined, tried and tested.

'From the perspectives of the rural residents, the educated youth had a good life. They did not have to work as hard as the local farmers and they had state and family subsidies.'

1967 CE

Foot-and-Mouth: In October, a vet first confirmed a sow in England had the disease; in total, there were about 2,200 confirmed cases of foot-and-mouth in the North-West Midlands and North Wales where livestock farming was most intense. The epidemic lasted 32 weeks, and ended with a total of 434,000 animals being slaughtered. Stricter controls on animal import and hygiene were enforced and there was not another major epidemic of foot-and-mouth until 2001, when 4 million animals were slaughtered in the UK.

1968 CE

The Club of Rome: Founded in Rome, Italy, the Club of Rome is self-described as 'a group of world citizens, sharing a common concern for the future of humanity'. The Club is made up of an international group of heads of states, high-level politicians and officials, scientists, economists, and others. In 1972, the group came to the fore with its seminal report *The Limits to Growth*. This was a book warning that if the world's consumption and population growth continued to aggressively increase, the earth would hit its saturation point for being able to support such growth. The underlying message was that this situation could be changed if people changed. The book was translated into 37 languages, and has sold more than 12 million copies worldwide. From *The First Global Revolution* (1993):

'The common enemy of humanity is man. In searching for a new enemy to unite us, we came up with the idea that pollution, the threat of global warming, water shortages, famine and the like would fit the bill. All these dangers are caused by human intervention, and it is only through changed attitudes and behavior that they can be overcome. The real enemy then, is humanity itself.'

1973 CE

Loi Royer (Royer Law): This law, passed in France, limited the physical size of some businesses. Among other provisions, it required a special permit for businesses larger than 1000 square meters in towns with fewer than 40,000 residents, and 1500 square meters in larger towns. The intent was to protect small grocers from supermarkets, which were thought to be encroaching at the time. The law had the effect of reducing competition in the retail sector in France.

1976 CE

High Fructose Corn Syrup: HFCS was first introduced in 1957, though the inventors were unsuccessful in mass producing the sticky syrup. The industrial production process and creation was made between 1965–1970 and was rapidly introduced to many processed foods and soft drinks in the US from about 1975 to 1985. In 1984, both Coke and Pepsi announced plans to switch from the more expensive sugar to HFCS in their drinks. US sugar consumption decreased by more than 500,000 tons a year.

1977 CE

IFAD: After the 1974 World Food Conference addressed the famine issues, focusing especially on Bangladesh, the UN developed the International Fund for Agricultural Development (IFAD). IFAD is a specialized agency established as an international financial institution in 1977 in response to the food crises of the early 1970s. What came out of the conference was that 'an International Fund for Agricultural Development should be established immediately to finance agricultural development projects primarily for food production in the developing countries'. Working with the community as participants, IFAD focuses on solutions tailored to the country, which may involve a number of activities, including increasing access to markets, technology and natural resources.

1978 CE

Permaculture: In response to the use of productionist agriculture practices, Bill Mollison and David Holmgren began to work on the concept of permaculture. They created a design that was published in *Permaculture One*, and described a system of sustainable human habitats that followed nature. Permaculture is based on a foundation of three core values, or ethics, as follows:

1. Care of the Earth: Provision for all life systems to continue and multiply.
2. Care of People: Provision for people to access those resources necessary for their existence.
3. Setting Limits to Population and Consumption: By governing our own needs, we can set resources aside to further the above principles.

1979 CE

Nutri-Matic: Individualized attention gets a whole new meaning in Douglas Adams' *The Hitchhiker's Guide to the Galaxy* where the Nutri-Matic drink dispenser determines your favourite drink.

'Arthur Dent has had a difficult day. Perhaps a beverage?'

'He had found a Nutri-Matic machine which had provided him with a plastic cup filled with a liquid that was almost, but not quite, entirely unlike tea. The way it functioned was very interesting. When the Drink button was pressed it made an instant but highly detailed examination of the subject's taste buds, a spectroscopic examination of the subject's metabolism and then sent tiny experimental signals down the neural pathways to the taste centers of the subject's brain to see what was likely to go down well. However, no one knew quite why it did this because it invariably delivered a cupful of liquid that was almost, but not quite, entirely unlike tea.'

1986 CE

Slow Food: When McDonald's opened in Turin, Italian Carlo Petrini founded Slow Food to promote an alternative to fast food. The organization strives to preserve traditional and regional cuisine and encourages farming of plants, seeds, and livestock that are culturally appropriate and characteristic of local ecosystems. Slow Food has grown to include over 150 countries, and includes a youth movement which aims to bring young artisans together with mentors to keep traditional foods and techniques being made.

1988 CE

Island in the Net: This 1988 science fiction novel by Bruce Sterling gives a view of the 21st century, where the world is peaceful with delocalized networking corporations. In the book, future food is artificial, called 'scop', which is a protein grown in vats. The protein can be made into any number of other products, as illustrated throughout the book.

'David was a health-food nut, a great devotee of unnatural foods. After eight years of marriage, Laura was used to it. At least the tech was improving. Even the scop, single-cell protein, was better these days. It tasted all right, if you could forget the image of protein vats crammed with swarming bacteria.'

'The poor lived cheap these days. Low-grade scop, fresh from the vats and dried like cornmeal, cost only a few cents a pound. Everyone in the ghetto suburbs ate scop, single-cell protein. The national food of the Third World.'

1994 CE

Flavr Savr Tomatoes: The first commercially grown genetically modified food is grown after FDA approval. While not a huge success, this did pave the way for approval – and disapproval – of other genetically modified crops.

1995 CE

WTO: The World Trade Organization was created in 1995 to supervise and liberalize international trade. The organization provides a framework for negotiating and formalizing trade agreements in adherence to WTO agreements by participating countries. The framework is based on five principles: non-discrimination, reciprocity, binding and enforceable commitments, transparency, and safety valves. Critics of the WTO suggest that smaller countries have little influence, and that most interest is focused on commercial profit-making companies; that labour and environment are ignored; and that the decision-making process is oversimplified and ineffective. Meetings, which take place every two years, have been bombarded with protestors, most notably in 1999 in Seattle, where 50,000 called for an end to globalization.

1995 CE

Oil for Food: UN programme established to allow Iraq to sell oil in exchange for food and other commodities.

1996 CE

Dolly the Sheep: At the Roslin Institute in Edinburgh scientists successfully clone the first mammal, resulting in a sheep named Dolly. Some herald this as the greatest scientific breakthrough of the decade, saying it will lead the way to study genetic diseases, while critics debate the ethical implications and declare it highly inefficient. Dolly died at the age of six of progressive lung disease; most sheep have a life expectancy between 10 to 12 years.

2001 CE

Square Fruit: Because of burgeoning populations, and lack of space, Japan begins marketing a square watermelon, with other square fruits, to fit conveniently in small refrigerators of small city apartments.

2002 CE

General Principles of Food Law: The European Commission entered this policy for the EU laying down general principles of food law, establishing the European Food Safety Authority (EFSA), and putting in place procedures for food safety. This law recognizes the rights of consumers to safe food and honest information, and establishes the principles, definitions and requirements for future food law in Europe. Beyond consumer welfare, the law takes aim at animal, plant, and environment health as well. This quote from the European Commission's objectives states:

"The food law aims at ensuring a high level of protection of human life and health, taking into account the protection of animal health and welfare, plant health and the environment. This integrated "farm to fork" approach is now considered a general principle for EU food safety policy.'

2003 CE

Custom-Made Chickens: Margaret Atwood, Canadian novelist and environmental activist, wrote about chickens grown for parts in her novel *Oryx and Crake*. Currently, chickens are being designed to go from chick to full-grown bird in shorter times with much larger breast pieces.

"What they were looking at was a large bulblike object that seemed to be covered with stippled whitish-yellow skin. Out of it came twenty thick fleshy tubes, and at the end of each tube another bulb was growing.

"What the hell is it?" said Jimmy.

"Those are chickens," said Crake. "Chicken parts. Just the breasts, on this one. They've got ones that specialize in drumsticks too, twelve to a growth unit."

"But there aren't any heads…"

"That's the head in the middle," said the woman. "There's a mouth opening at the top, they dump nutrients in there. No eyes or beak or anything, they don't need those."

2003 CE

Fome Zero: Fome Zero, or Zero Hunger, is a Brazilian strategy by the federal government to put into action the right of access to basic food. The strategy is mixed with food and nutrition security, social inclusion and citizen rights for the poorest populations. This became the first time food security was priority in social policy in Brazil, and is still in effect today. Several programmes are run under the strategy to strengthen family agriculture, income generation, access to foods, and society mobilization. Examples of programme initiatives included scholarships for families conditional upon school attendance, hot meals provided at schools, local contracts with farmers providing direct links to schools and other community outlets, distribution of supplements, and creating low-cost restaurants.

2005 CE

La Londonisation: Paris Mayor Bertrand Delanoe lays out plans for Paris to avoid 'La Londonisation' of Paris, his catchall phrase for the rubber stamp commoditizing of the High Street, ruin of small businesses, and driving out of the middle classes to the suburbs. He promised more affordable housing and a law banning

Locavore: In response to ever-lengthening food miles, locavores emerged (and the word was made official by *New Oxford American Dictionary* in 2007) as concerned foodies who make a conscious effort to eat within 100-mile radius of where they live. It started with a group of concerned bloggers in the San Francisco area, but now the movement – unlike its message – has gone global.

2006 CE

London Food Strategy: In 2006, the first Mayor of London, Ken Livingstone, launched a strategy to improve London's food and reduce environmental impact of the food industry. This was the first strategy of its type, especially for a city of its size, and the plan to improve Londoners' health through better diet by increasing the choice, availability and quality of food for all was an ambitious one. The strategy was based on five themes: to improve health through food, reduce the negative environmental impacts of food, support a vibrant food economy, celebrate and promote London's diverse food scene, and develop London's food security for all, especially the most disadvantaged. Proposed initiatives included developing training courses for catering in schools and elsewhere on sourcing local supplies of healthy foods, supporting local food companies through events and awards, communicating nutrition messages, and developing a brand to note local foods in markets.

2008 CE

Rice Shortage: The price of rice, a staple in the diets of nearly half the world's population, has almost doubled on international markets since the New Year began. This has affected the budget – and nutrition – of millions of under-served Asians and ultimately many others, and began an intense year of restrictions, rationing, and riots. National governments, such as India, Cambodia, and Egypt began restricting export of rice, while retailers began rationing sales due to fears of insufficient global supplies. In April, prices for rice doubled (hitting $0,24/pound). Countries such as India, China, Bangladesh, Philippines and Thailand felt the increase immediately; only Japan, which produces enough of its own rice to meet domestic demand, maintained prices without concern. Outside of Asia, other countries felt it too: in Haiti riots erupted over the rising price of this staple.

Global Seed Bank: Jokingly called the Apocalyptic seed bank, the Svalbard Global Seed Vault, a secure seed bank on a remote Norwegian Island, is definitely no joke. The seeds, donated from all over the world, are stored in a vault in the side of an Arctic mountain ready to be re-sewn in the case of global catastrophe. Storage of seeds is free, and seeds remain the property of the donating country. The vault can hold up to 4,5 million batches of seeds, making it possible to re-establish plants if they were to vanish from existence. And, even if there is fallout – and the bank loses power – the climate should keep them safe for several thousand years. Plenty of time to fix those power lines.

2009 CE

Safety Pact: China, Japan, and South Korea sign a food safety pact in the wake of concerns over pesticide-contaminated Chinese-made dumplings that affected 10 people in Japan. Health ministers from all three countries signed an accord in Tokyo agreeing to notify each other immediately if a food safety problem arises, for a discussion and clarification of the investigation process; all three also stand together on the fight against swine flu.

2010 CE

The Vertical Farm:
Though the term 'vertical farming' was coined in 1915 by Gilbert Ellis Bailey, the book *The Vertical Farm* by Dickson Despommier has excited scientists, architects, and politicians around the globe. He recommends farms grown inside skyscrapers, which could provide alleviation from the upcoming issue of how to feed the ever-growing population. The hydroponic system would allow year-round production, urban growing, immunity to weather-related crop failure, and sustainable processes, not to mention changing the way we use pesticides and fertilizers. And the vertical farms built in cities would create new ways of earning for both skilled and unskilled laborers. Critics still cite the need for traditional agriculture as a way to preserve animal life, and preserve endangered species. In the original book *Vertical Farming* (1915), Gilbert Ellis Bailey describes a vertical farm that goes down instead of up:

"'Vertical Farming", to coin a name, is the keynote of a new agriculture that has come to stay, for inexpensive explosives enable the farmer to farm deeper, to go down to increase his acreage, and to secure larger crops. Instead of spreading out over more land he concentrates on less land and becomes an intensive rather than an extensive agriculturist, and soon learns that it is more profitable to double the depth of his fertile land than to double the area of his holdings, and he learns that his best aid and servant in this work is a good explosive. Peace congresses demand that words be turned into pruning hooks. The farmer is busy turning explosives from war to agriculture, from death dealing to life giving work.'

2012–2017 CE

Food Tubes:
Cutting down on emissions from highways caused by our globalized food system, Food Tubes brings the idea of an underground 'internet' of sorts, tubes twisting and intertwining through cities, and eventually out into the countryside as well. The tubes are powered by air pressure or linear induction motors, and the vehicles (large capsules) will transport our food underground, reducing the carbon footprint, and thus cutting our dependence on gas. Foodtubes hopes to test the system first, and then try it out in the United Kingdom. CEO Noel Hodson of Foodtubes predicts an operational 100 kilometer food tube circuit in a rural area within five years, and in a dense urban area within ten.

2013 CE

Lab-Grown Burger: Dutch-born Willem van Eelen came up with the idea of lab-grown meat after being haunted with thoughts of starvation and animal abuse from his time in POW camps during World War II. The idea was put into motion when Van Eelen, with a large grant from the Dutch government gathered scientists from Amsterdam, Utrecht, and Eindhoven to work toward making this a reality. The idea was out there, and now another Dutchman is taking over as Mark Post, vascular biologist at the University of Maastricht, has stated in interviews that he thinks a lab-grown hamburger can be produced – at a hefty cost – within the next year. And, he's got a grant to back him up. In-vitro meat is made by placing cells into nutrients that can help them thrive. The growing tissue is stretched and moulded into food, which can then (presumably) be cooked and eaten like any other meat or processed meat. Growing in-vitro meat would not only help to alleviate the stress in hungry countries, but could have positive impacts on the environment, as raising animals is extremely intensive in resource usage, and of course detrimental to their welfare.

2022 CE

3D Printer Food: Though 3D printers aren't the latest component, it is the 'growing' or creation of edible foodstuff that makes this printer being designed at MIT remarkable. The machine prints food using multiple cartridges with edible inks and electronic blueprints. The inks go line by line to create a desired shape. Advocates tout it as a way to create food not only for people who won't or can't cook for themselves, but also as a way to create foodstuff packed with nutrients to be shipped to countries in need. Furthermore, the number of hands involved in the food's production greatly decreases, as there is minimal preparation and shipping. So far, the printer has been successful at printing chocolates, cookies, cheese, dough, and even protein. Critics are sceptical that the food will actually taste good, comparing it to the MREs served to the military.

2050 CE

Dongtan: All eyes are on China, a country that's no stranger to rapid development, as they work to open Dongtan, an eco-city near Shanghai that was first presented at the United Nations World Urban Forum. Though started in 2005, the project has hit some obstacles, and the new completion date has been moved to 2050. The city is meant to be self-sufficient in water and energy, and wind turbines have supposedly been built. Most of the city's waste will be recycled and used as a resource, and cars may be subjected to out-of-city parking.

Foodprint: Artistic Reflections on Practical Issues[1]

The Curator
Peter de Rooden

'How can art influence the future of our food?' is the initial question of the three-year programme *Foodprint. Food for the City* in Stroom Den Haag. Dutch curator and artist Peter de Rooden reflects on the role of artists, designers and architects in the debate about the future of food in the city.

Thirty years ago, the American artist Agnes Denes created an iconic work of land art: *Wheatfield – A Confrontation*. It was a golden field of wheat, situated between the famous skyscrapers of Manhattan and the Statue of Liberty, near the New York Stock Exchange. Denes's artwork made the public aware of how important food is to cities like New York; and it is as topical now as it was in 1982, when the wheat was first sown and harvested. Basically, cities are giants with feet of clay: without basic products such as grain, their ingenious machinery would grind to a halt. In a sense, *Edible Park* is an heir to *Wheatfield*, perhaps less iconic but no less radical.

In the past few years, food as a lifestyle theme has become extremely popular, evidenced by celebrity chefs on television, dieting trends, hip movements like 'guerrilla gardening' and 'slow food', and growing your own vegetables again. At the same time, it is obvious that there is a wide gap between where our food comes from and where it is eaten, between origin and plate, between city and countryside. The journey from the fields and the sea to our plates has become a long, complex and global one.

In the industrialized cities of the western world, food production has gradually become invisible over the course of just the past few generations, as illustrated in Carolyn Steel's *Hungry City*. The rising value of urban soil has moved allotment gardens to the edges of cities. Cattle markets are no longer held in inner cities, and how many people still have a pig in their backyard? In urban planning, food is a non-item. Often, architects only design spatial or logistic solutions to accommodate shops, supermarkets, and the supply of produce and removal of waste – also because their clients do not ask them for anything else. Public parks and gardens consist of cheap and maintenance-free 'visual green'.

All this raises questions about food security. What if, through some crisis or other, our supermarkets were no longer supplied? There are numerous developments – such as climate change, energy scarcity, population growth, food speculation – that make guaranteeing a sufficient, healthy, and sustainable food supply in the coming decades a serious task indeed. Experts from various disciplines are racking their brains over this, and many reports are produced. Meanwhile, novels such as Margaret Atwood's *The Year of the Flood* (2009) or a recent film such as Steven Soderbergh's *Contagion* present us with a frightening image of a future in which food is no longer a matter of course, not even for Westerners.

Not only novelists and filmmakers contemplate the future of our food. For artists, designers, autonomous architects, and cultural institutes, food is an important theme.[2] What does working and thinking from within the arts contribute to addressing the food issue?

Foodprint. Food for the City

In answering that question, the experiences of the long-range programme *Foodprint. Food for the City* initiated by Stroom Den Haag provide some interesting reference material. *Foodprint*, running from the spring of 2009 until early 2012, included a wide range of activities and events for both professionals and the wider audience: exhibitions, lectures, a festival, design projects, art projects in public space, research, closed expert meetings, and publications. Stroom's policy focuses on the city and the urban condition, whereby the disciplines of art, design, and architecture are at once starting points and tools for addressing urban and social themes. The theme of food presented itself to Stroom as a result of the growing social and artistic interest it had generated. Food soon turned out to be a very interesting way of looking at the planning and functioning of cities.

For *Foodprint*, Stroom therefore took as its main starting point the question of how a city like The Hague could re-establish the link between city dwellers and their food sources. The study 'Food for the City', carried out by Stroom in 2010 on behalf of InnovationNetwork, showed where, how, for whom, and especially in collaboration with which parties, food production in The Hague may be meaningful. Elements that popped up were, for instance, closing local cycles, waste management, reducing food miles and CO_2 emissions, countering heat stress resulting from buildings and asphalt, and providing healthy recreational facilities, social meeting points, and education – but also guaranteeing food security and promoting self-sufficiency in city dwellers.

While this urban food production features prominently in a number of projects that have been presented or developed within the framework of *Foodprint*, the artists, designers, and architects also addressed quite different issues. Some of them have, for instance, confronted us with our preconceived notions and assumptions about food, while others placed more emphasis on developing practical, feasible alternatives, and still others experimented with food in the public domain.

Looking from a New Angle

During the opening exhibition of *Foodprint* in 2009, Joep van Lieshout caused quite a commotion with his dystopian work *Foodmaster*. Visitors entered a three-dimensional installation, consisting of an abattoir and industrial machines, in which people were processed into pig feed and other products. Van Lieshout's reasoning is as straightforward as it is radical: only by making humans part of the industrial food system can we save both humanity and our planet. At first sight, the colouring book of a modern pig farm by the designer Christien Meindertsma seemed much friendlier. But on closer examination, it ruthlessly overturned the romantic urban stereotype of farms with thatched roofs, chickens in the yard, and pigs rooting about in the mud.

At the exhibition *Food Forward* in the spring of 2012, Arne Hendriks presented his project *The Incredible Shrinking Man*. How would our footprint on this planet change if, instead of growing larger and larger, we reversed the trend and shrank people to roughly 50 centimetres in height? Hendriks plays with scale, compelling us to think about human impact on the earth. Artist John O'Shea's *Black Market Pudding* is as stimulating as it is controversial. What if we drew blood from living animals to make products like black pudding? Then the animals would not have to be slaughtered but could lead good lives, and we could go on eating meat products.

Alternatives for the Future

Foodprint worked with two architectural offices on very practical and potentially feasible alternatives for the future of our food. Winy Maas and the Why Factory, his think tank at Delft University of Technology, were invited to carry out the project *City Pig*, designing a socially and ecologically responsible and economically viable organic pig farm in the city.[3] How can pigs, which have lived in cities for centuries, return there, where most meat consumers live? Is it conceivable that livestock could be raised and meat produced in The Hague? How could this benefit city-dwellers, businesses, and animals?

The *City Pig* design proposals provoked vehement reactions from the city authorities, farmers, and urbanites, despite their undeniable contribution to animal welfare and a more sustainable city. They involved recycling local food waste by using it as pig feed, thereby producing meat more efficiently; supplying 5,100 households with energy through manure fermentation; and drastically reducing food miles through local slaughter and the use of food waste as feed. On 27 June 2009, the Agrarisch Dagblad, a newspaper for the Dutch agricultural sector, ran an article with the head-line 'Veehouderij in de stad is brug te ver' (Raising livestock in the city is a bridge too far), in which an alderman of The Hague argued for strict separation of the city and countryside: 'There's a reason people choose to live in the city.'

The design proposal for *Park Supermarket* by Van Bergen Kolpa Architects[4] for a food production landscape between The Hague and Rotterdam proved to be equally controversial. The idea was triggered by the national 'Randstad 2040' strategy, which mentions the construction of metropolitan landscape parks with a recreational function for the urban population. Van Bergen Kolpa wondered whether the design of these parks could reflect the fact that they are partly located on agricultural land. In other words, is it possible for an area to be attractive for recreation, appealing as a landscape, and productive as well?

The design proposed that most of what a modern supermarket has on its shelves be grown at an easily accessible place in one of the intended landscape park locations in Midden-Delfland (a green area of South Holland's Westland region). Besides traditional Dutch products, wild rice, olives, avocados, and coffee beans could also be grown there. Critics of the idea envisioned an artificial, far-fetched, and functional landscape that would hardly evoke memories of the original 'polder' land-scape. But what is 'far-fetched' here? To use tax money to preserve a 17th-century Dutch polder landscape and meanwhile import green beans from Africa, or to grow rice on our own soil and respond to our current eating habits? Although the proposal was exhibited around the world, neither it nor City Pig will become a reality in the Netherlands any time soon.

Out of the City, into the Neighbourhoods

In 2010, Stroom commissioned two art projects in public space [5]: *Edible Park* and *Foodscape Schilderswijk*. Both address issues of urban food production and expand the concept of art in public space through their protean nature and the involvement of local residents and neighbourhood organizations. These are not finished works, installed fully formed in the middle of an urban neighbourhood, but social sculptures that invite participation by local residents, sculptures that grow and (in these cases) are edible.

With *Edible Park*, the British artist Nils Norman tests in practice whether permaculture, a design method that has its roots in utopian notions, could lead to a different way of planning and developing modern cities. The project includes two permaculture gardens and a sustainable pavilion that can accommodate meetings and activities.[6] Norman sees utopian models such as permaculture not only as alternatives that improve society, but also as lenses through which modern society can be examined critically. *Foodscape Schilderswijk*, by the American/Dutch artist Debra Solomon, is also founded on a utopian vision.[7] In the socially disadvantaged and very much built-up Schilderswijk neighbourhood of The Hague, Solomon wants to create a green infrastructure consisting of sustainable edible greenery, such as fruit trees and nut trees, berry bushes, artichokes, and various herbs. With *Foodscape*, Solomon aims to contribute to a healthier ecosystem and better living conditions in this neighbourhood. *Foodscape* presents an alternative to the traditional layout of public and green spaces in cities like The Hague by replacing visual green with edible greens.

Conclusions

To return to our earlier question: What can art mean to the future of our food? Stroom's *Foodprint* programme and the response it has solicited underscore the fact that food is so much more than just a basic necessity of life. How we grow, prepare, and eat our food is strongly interwoven with our culture, the society we live in, and how we see ourselves. So of course we eat mangoes in the winter and red cabbage salad in the summer, and of course we want to have meat every day but no cattle in the city; we have come to find eating horseflesh unthinkable and drink expensive fruit juice simply because we believe in 'super fruits'. Issues related to food demand solutions on many levels: technology, administration, economy, design, legislation, culture, and society. However, new approaches only tend to work if they are accepted on both an emotional and rational level.

Art has the ability to undermine our preconceived notions and ossified images and to show alternatives. Art puts different questions to us than the ones policymakers or people working in the food industry are capable of asking. Artists address problems in the domains of food and urban planning from an autonomous position, not beholden to economic and administrative interests of the food sector. This makes it possible for them to establish contact between parties that would normally not sit down together. 'It's precisely by asking questions that are never asked in the sector that [Stroom's Foodprint programme] opens people's eyes',[8] said Hiske Ridder of InnovationNetwork.

This raises the thorny question of the value and significance of art in relation to social issues. Opening people's eyes is not the same as putting ideas into practice. The *Foodprint* programme had an impact, as 'proved' by thick folders of newspaper clippings, high visitor numbers, and enthusiastic responses. Yet, with some frustration, we must observe that pigs have not yet moved into the city in significant numbers, and that rice and avocados have yet to take root in the Dutch polders. Artists, architects, and designers have presented alternatives; now it is up to us to take them seriously. It hardly seems probable that the future food scenarios dished out by multinationals, politicians, or food producers will be palatable to us. Those parties have other interests than a responsibly filled belly: profit maximization, shareholder value, market percentage, and political capital.

Financial Support for Farmers

Average financial support (% of gross farm receipts) paid to farmers in different countries in the periods 2007-2009. Future developments will depend on policy decisions.

Source: OECD, *Agricultural policies in OECD countries at a glance 2010* (Paris: OECD Publishing, 2010)

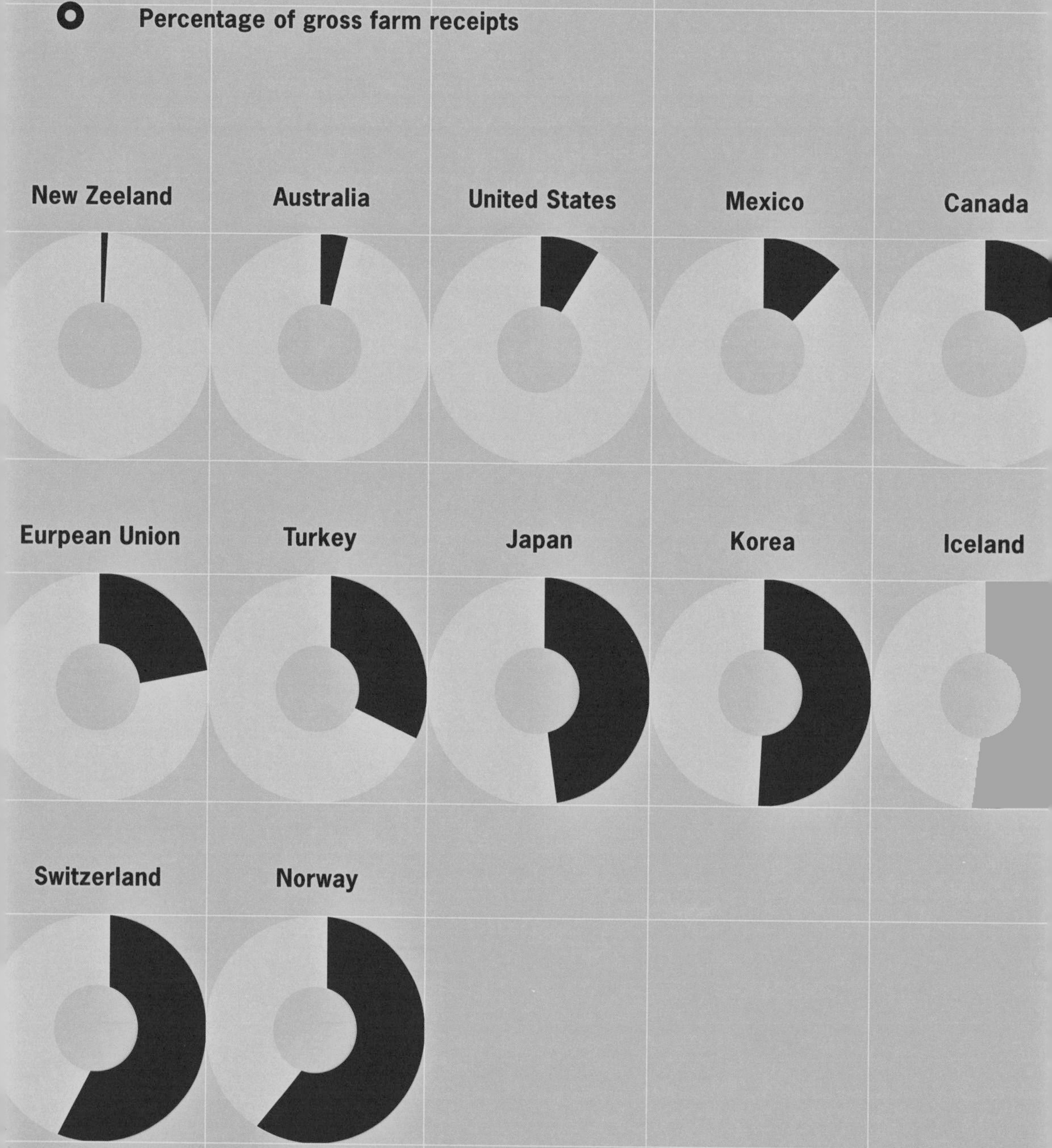

◉ **Percentage of gross farm receipts**

New Zeeland

Australia

United States

Mexico

Canada

Eurpean Union

Turkey

Japan

Korea

Iceland

Switzerland

Norway

Genetically Engineered Seeds: A Monopoly

Percentage of genetically engineered seeds owned by countries and multinationals.

Source: Online. Available http://www.greenpeace.nl/campaigns/gentech/ (accessed 1 February 2012).

● **Percentage owned by countries**

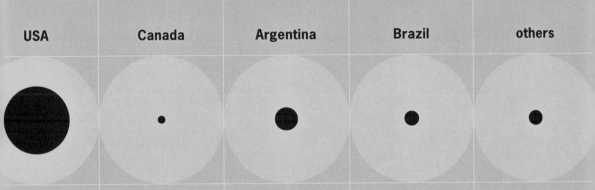

USA	Canada	Argentina	Brazil	others

○ **Percentage owned by Monsato**
◉ **Percentage owned by Syngenta, Dupont, Bayer and other**

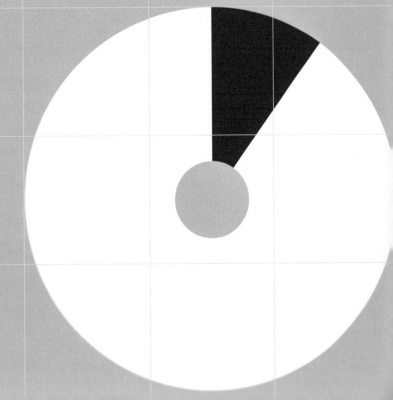

Seed

43

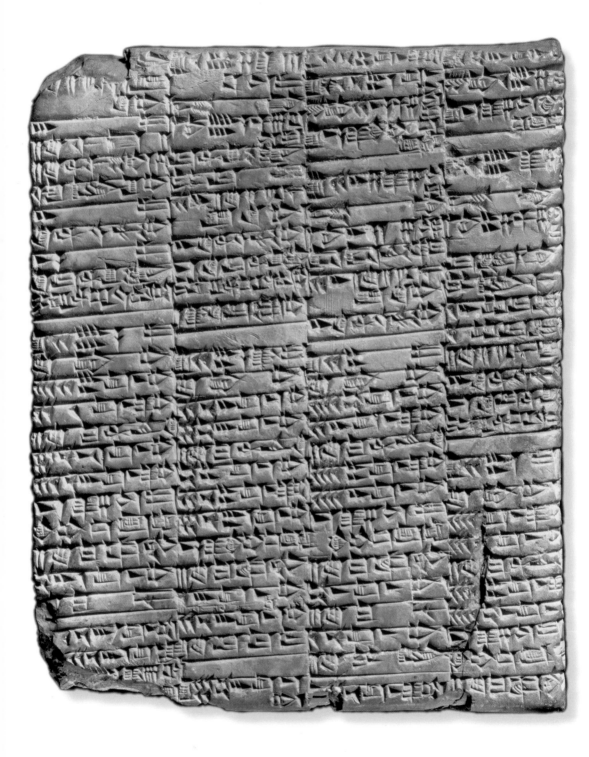

Code		Species		Origin Geographic	Harvest D	No./seeds	Germination (%)
NGA057	14			United State of	12/1/2004	250	90
NGA057	14			Ghana	12/1/2004	250	90
NGA057	14			South Africa	1/1/2004	250	90
NGA057	14			Botswana	1/1/2005	250	90
NGA057	14			United State of	9/1/2005	250	90
NGA057	14			Uganda	9/1/2005	250	90
NGA057	14	Cowpea	1418	Vigna	unguiculata	Uruguay	12/1/2004	250	90
NGA057	14	Cowpea	1429	Vigna	unguiculata	Indonesia	1/1/2005	250	90
NGA057	14	Cowpea	1445	Vigna	unguiculata	India	12/1/2004	250	90
NGA057	14	Cowpea	1560	Vigna	unguiculata	Turkey	12/1/2004	250	90
NGA057	14	Cowpea	1674	Vigna	unguiculata	Ghana	1/1/2004	250	90
NGA057	14	Cowpea	1709	Vigna	unguiculata	United State of	12/1/2004	250	90
NGA057	14	Cowpea	1756	Vigna	unguiculata	Kenya	12/1/2004	250	90
NGA057	14	Cowpea	1766	Vigna	unguiculata	Pakistan	12/1/2004	250	90
NGA057	14	Cowpea	1775	Vigna	unguiculata	Israel	1/1/2005	250	90
NGA057	14	Cowpea	1828	Vigna	unguiculata	Iran	12/1/2004	250	90
NGA057	14	Cowpea	1832	Vigna	unguiculata	Puerto Rico	1/1/2005	250	90
NGA057	14	Cowpea	1861	Vigna	unguiculata	Pakistan	11/1/2004	250	90
NGA057	14	Cowpea	1872	Vigna	unguiculata	United State of	2/1/2005	250	90
NGA057	14	Cowpea	1874	Vigna	unguiculata	United Kingdom	9/1/2005	250	90
NGA057	14	Cowpea	1878	Vigna	unguiculata	United Kingdom	1/1/2005	250	90
NGA057	14	Cowpea	1880	Vigna	unguiculata	Guatemala	1/1/2005	250	90
NGA057	14	Cowpea	1891	Vigna	unguiculata	El Salvador	1/1/2005	250	90
NGA057	14	Cowpea	1916	Vigna	unguiculata	Hungary	9/1/2005	250	90
NGA057	14	Cowpea	1933	Vigna	unguiculata	Iran	12/1/2004	250	90
NGA057	14	Cowpea	1947	Vigna	unguiculata	South Africa	12/1/2004	250	90
NGA057	14	Cowpea	1980	Vigna	unguiculata	Nigeria	11/1/2004	250	90
NGA057	14	Cowpea	1982	Vigna	unguiculata	Argentina	11/1/2004	250	90
NGA057	14	Cowpea	2009	Vigna	unguiculata	Hungary	1/1/2005	250	90
NGA057	14	Cowpea	2037	Vigna	unguiculata	Argentina	1/1/2005	250	90
NGA057	14	Cowpea	2051	Vigna	unguiculata	Nigeria	1/1/2006	250	90
NGA057	14	Cowpea	2085	Vigna	unguiculata	United State of	9/1/2005	250	90
GA057	14	Cowpea	2094	Vigna	unguiculata	United State of	1/1/2005	250	90
GA057	14	Cowpea	2103	Vigna	unguiculata	United State of	9/1/2005	250	90
A057	14	Cowpea	2111	Vigna	unguiculata	United State of	9/1/2005	250	90
A057	14	Cowpea	2128	Vigna	unguiculata	United State of	9/1/2005	250	90
057	14	Cowpea	2136	Vigna	unguiculata	United State of	9/1/2005	250	90
57	14	Cowpea	2179	Vigna	unguiculata	India	9/1/2005	250	90
57	14	Cowpea	2267	Vigna	unguiculata	Colombia	1/1/2005	250	90
57	14	Cowpea	2276	Vigna	unguiculata	Paraguay	12/1/2004	250	90

page 54

A lab technician takes samples from eggs at a laboratory in Bangkok after a deadly strain of bird flu has broken out in Thailand. The deadly H5N1 strain of the virus was detected in chickens and fighting cocks in eight provinces.

Photo: Saeed Khan. Source: Food and Agriculture Organization in the series 'Towards a more sustainable livestock sector'

page 55

Food security concerns in sub-Saharan countries stimulate the use of any technology that will enhance production without jeopardizing trade. Corporate and public researchers join hands in the development of genetically modified corn varieties suitable for local conditions, in this case in Kenya.

Photo: Dave Hoisington. Source: CIMMYT

page 56 top

The Svalbard Global Seed Vault, a global 'central bank' for the world's seeds (primarily of food plants) in the permafrost of Norway, preserves the world's biodiversity, adapting to climate change and global warming and thereby ensuring food for the world's population for the foreseeable future. This photo shows the front entrance of the seed bank with the light art work by the Norwegian artist Dyveke Sannes.

Photo: Mari Tefre. Source: Svalbard Global Seed Vault

page 56 bottom

Svalbard boxes ready for shipment. Each shipment/storage box contains the list of accessions with minimum germplasm data (institute code, accessions number, scientific and common name, number of seeds per pack, year of regeneration, country of origin). The Seed Vault has the capacity to store 4,5 million different seed samples. Each sample will contain on average 500 seeds, so a maximum of 2,25 billion seeds may be stored in the Seed Vault.

Photo: The International Institute of Tropical Agriculture in Nigeria (IITA). Source: Svalbard Global Seed Vault

Food, A Compromised Issue

The Philosopher
Huub Dijstelbloem

According to the American writer Jonathan Saffran Foer, eating is farming by proxy. The Dutch lecturer in Philosophy of Science at the University of Amsterdam and Senior Researcher at the Scientific Council for Government Policy in The Hague (WRR) Huub Dijstelbloem points out that this metaphor may be appealing, but is also misleading.

Farming by Proxy

In his book *Eating Animals* (2009) the American writer Jonathan Saffran Foer, a convert to vegetarianism, goes in search of the moral aspects and significance of eating animals. When Foer visits the farm of Paul Willis in Thornton, Iowa, his host quotes the American farmer and man of letters Wendell Berry: 'Every time you make a decision about food, you are farming by proxy.' Foer is telling us that every time a person makes a decision about food he is operating a kind of long-distance fork that influences what types of food are produced and how. To him, awareness of what you choose to eat is a moral duty.

As spoken by the farmer in Foer's book, Wendell Berry's words are almost a throwaway line. But if eating is farming by proxy, then consumers are wielding some awfully heavy silverware. Berry made this claim as part of a debate with American conservationists. Historically and culturally, American intellectuals since Thoreau seem to have been more interested in wilderness and how they can protect it than in what happens on farms. They resolve the conflict between culture and nature by leaving the former (in many cases the city) and settling in the latter, often in the form of a barely inhabitable wasteland. This solution is too simplistic for Berry, however. Between nature and culture lies our food. It strikes him as absurd to think about food without pausing to consider how it is produced. Therein lies the explanation of his statement that 'eating is an agricultural act'.

Food Networks

The main point of this essay is that the metaphor of farming by proxy is appealing but also misleading. Although intended to add an ethical dimension to the agency of food consumers, the image has unfortunate side effects. Anyone who eats – and who doesn't? – must choose, select, determine their preferences and priorities, Foer says. For him, food is a moral issue, and what we eat can no longer be decided in splendid isolation. But is eating really farming by proxy, or does this exaggerate and overemphasize the personal aspect of consuming food, defining it too glibly as a 'political' matter?

Foer wades, probably unintentionally, into a classic sociological debate, inadvertently doing justice to the title of his novel *Extremely Loud and Incredibly Close*. He raises the question of how the micro and macro levels are interrelated. In the case of food, micro and macro are linked, in that private and existential pleasures have become a global issue. That does not mean that food is now suddenly a worldwide concern – it already has been for some time. It does suggest, however, that one feature of globalization is that the chains and networks connecting people are becoming longer, and that the personal and political are ever more closely linked, because it is also becoming easier to make those chains visible.

Science and technology are making the intimate connection between the local and the global increasingly explicit by providing greater insights into causal relationships and identifying externalities. Take 'the climate', for example, which in the space of a few decades, despite its enormous complexity, has become a more or less measurable system (or at least one that can be monitored). An organization has even emerged that acts as a mouthpiece for the climate, namely the IPCC (Inter-governmental Panel on Climate Change).

Food, like the climate, is 'extremely loud and incredibly close'. When an issue presents itself in global terms, as climate change does, people become companions in distress. The problems affecting them make them partners in adversity, facing a challenge that spills over doorsteps and national borders. They involuntarily participate in a problem that goes to the heart of a society's economic development, one with both a strong sociopolitical dimension and an existential character, in that it is bound up with the way our lives are organized today.

But their participation in the problem does not imply direct relationships between the local and global. Rather, those relationships involve numerous forms of mediation: the media, in the broadest sense, as well as measurement systems, transport vehicles, infrastructures, information transfer, money, and countless intentional and unintentional consequences of human action. The food system is one manifestation of this type of transglobal network; it resembles a large-scale techno-scientific network by virtue of all the links in its complex chains.

Black Boxes

The weave of such networks, according to the French philosopher of science Bruno Latour in *Science in Action* (1987), is 'in a large part the history of the resources scattered along networks to accelerate the mobility, faithfulness, combination and cohesion of traces that make action at a distance possible'. Such systems owe their cohesiveness to their intermediate steps, yet ironically, they eliminate the traces of those steps at the end of the chain. Both scientists and food manufacturers prefer to present products (or facts) whose origins and histories have been effaced. The final result is a 'black box' that no longer reveals where it was made or what values, possibilities, limitations, and meanings were put inside it in the process. This has led supporters of the past Arts and Crafts Movement and the present Maker Movement, in their campaigns against the industrialization of the production and use of goods, to adopt the slogan, 'If you can't open it, you don't own it.'

The Food Movement, the contours of which are now visible in a wide range of initiatives around the globe, is doing something similar. Its members likewise seek to open the black box – not some machine or mass-produced designer product, but the food on our tables. In this respect, the food movement is reminiscent of the early days of the environmental movement; initially focused on practical, tangible problems such as pollution and foul smells, the movement became a forum for concerns about problems that transcend territorial and sectoral boundaries, culminating in the world-wide climate crisis.

The point about food is that opening the black box sets in motion a process that makes many things more *explicit*. It creates a kind of proximity between personal issues and global problems, making it ever harder to separate the two. Food makes the personal political and the political personal. The power of such problems – their integrative and inevitable, but also unsettling power – is that they interweave local and global issues. The chains become ever longer, more complex, and more vulnerable. They tie together very different fields, linking consumption and matters of taste with worldwide challenges such as water shortages, resource scarcity, the growing world population, and ongoing urbanization. Yet that link is not made directly but indirectly.

Between Farm and Fork

For some years now, the discontent resulting from these problems has led to a rise in citizen-consumer movements for more local, small-scale, organic food production. These demands for a smaller scale and greater sustainability are generally regarded as a tipping point in an ecological turn from large-scale food production to sustainable food systems.

The question, however, is whether changes in consumption patterns are really so directly related to changes in food production and distribution. Do the food movement's manoeuvres nudge major producers and retailers towards greater sustainability, or do retailers have reasons of their own for reforming the system, and are the slight shifts in consumer preferences no more than an epiphenomenon?

The different steps between the global and the local are not connected by one long cable but by a series of shorter strands knotted together: processing, transport, logistics, trade, and so forth. The long chains that connect rural food production to urban consumption run through all sorts of intermediate zones with their own values, cultures, traditions, orders, techniques, and legitimacy.

The outcome of thinking in linear relationships between farm and fork is that consumers come under moral pressure to make the world a better place through their personal choices, even though they have very limited means for action *within the chain*. Both factually and morally, farming by proxy is not a very constructive image.

What image might do more justice to reality and offer a more realistic moral perspective, not only to consumers but to all parties involved in food production?

Eating is an act that connects people. But this connection is not a logical series of steps in which a consumer item is first produced and later ends up in a supermarket in the city. At every step in the process the food is transformed, through practices that – although interrelated – each have their own internal form of rationality. A farmer, a halal butcher, a retailer, a food inspector, and your average carnivorous consumer all relate to the same 'object', meat, in different ways. Each of these individuals also justifies his or her attitude towards meat differently, as a producer, person of faith, citizen, employee, official, or consumer. This finds expression in a particular manner of speaking, a repertoire of ways to relate one's personal situation to a practice with its own tradition and legitimacy.

Collision and Compromise

In *On Justification: Economies of Worth* (2006), the French sociologist Luc Boltanski and economist Laurent Thévenot describe such intermediate stations as 'worlds'; the participants in these worlds, they argue, justify their actions by reference to their own principles of rationality. It is important to observe that these 'worlds of worth' are not always on friendly terms. More typically, their relations are marked by tension, friction, continuous conflict with opposing interests, and imperialistic tendencies. Consider the conflicts between economic interests and sustainability. Sometimes they can be reconciled, but sometimes they remain opposed and incompatible. They are 'worlds in collision'.

Such collisions can be prevented or resolved through 'compromise'. According to Boltanski and Thévenot, a compromise is an agreement between different worlds with the aim of preventing a collision, because a conflict cannot be resolved within a single world. The result is a new, composite world.

The relationship between food and consumers is one such compromise, as is the relationship between production and the environment, or between animal welfare and transport. But 'compromise' is no guarantee of perpetual peace; rather, the relationship is 'compromised' in both senses of the word. Eating, especially eating meat, is a compromising activity, because of its 'foodprint', its impact on scarce natural resources such as water, fertile soil, and the environment; it therefore necessitates compromises, because eating responsibly means finding one's way under suboptimal conditions.

In the collisions and compromises between worlds, food is brought into close contact with faraway things. This can again be illustrated by analogy with climate change, which is also too vast in many ways to admit of a coherent policy; the scale of the problem exceeds that of national legislatures, the problems are too heterogeneous in nature, the contributions to the cause are unequal, and different countries have differing levels of resources for solving the problem, financing solutions, enforcing compliance, etc. This is why more and more initiatives are coming into view that seek to identify the consequences of climate change at a smaller, local scale, for instance through alliances between states with similar problems that can benefit from sharing their knowledge and experience.

Boltanski and Thévenot's concept of multiple regimes of justification is a valuable way of lightening the moral burden that food consumption threatens to impose. Anyone who eats – and eats meat in particular – has the whole world on his or her plate, Foer tells us. This type of diagnosis places too heavy a burden on the consumer – a burden, moreover, which is not justified.

Food Out of the Black Box

A food chain connects nature and culture, country and city, agriculture and industry. But these stops along the way are not simply territorial in character. The route runs straight through a number of different regimes of justification. This makes eating much more than 'an agricultural act'. It is also a cultural and an industrial act – an act, moreover, that cannot be performed by a person acting alone (the consumer at the end of the chain) but involves many people and social practices with their own regimes of justification.

The 'compromise' necessary to bring about greater engagement with food issues cannot be found on the consumer's plate. It cannot be reached by moral deliberation on the consumer's part, the alternative choices and purchases to which this may lead, or the different messages that this will send along the supply chain. The compromises needed to mitigate the damage caused by food production (to resources, the environment, and animals) will have to be forged between different 'worlds', just as the problem of climate change cannot be solved either at the level of individual citizens or at the level of a collective global organization. It will require alliances between groups tackling similar problems and compromises in the face of competing issues.

This calls for a certain transparency, for clarification of the hidden trade-offs, invisible costs, and externalities that have not been factored into the equation (or for which some other party is expected to foot the bill). To achieve that, we must above all continue the process of making things explicit, of displaying the steps between farm and fork and revealing the colliding logics that are now sometimes veiled in compromises. Only by opening the black boxes can we make comparison possible, so that consumers can decide which compromises are and are not acceptable to them.

Finding Answers in the Rubble of Haiti

The Chef
José Andrés

The catastrophic earthquake that hit Haiti on January 12, 2010 killed 300,000 people and left another one million survivors homeless. Unexpectedly, chef and owner of the think tank *Think Food Group*, the Spanish/American José Andrés, discovers that the solution of our future global food problems lies in Haiti.

I arrived in Haiti on a rainy day in April 2010 to see what I, as a chef, could do to help after one of the worst natural disasters in the western hemisphere in living memory. Just three months earlier, a catastrophic earthquake had killed more than 300,000 people in one of the world's poorest nations and left another one million survivors homeless. It was hard at that time to imagine a worse food crisis anywhere on the planet.

I have long believed that chefs can work with communities to tackle big problems. My work with DC Central Kitchen in Washington showed me that food and cooking can do more than just feed the hungry. The Kitchen recycles food that would otherwise go to waste in the capital city of the world's biggest economy. But it also trains the unemployed and homeless the skills they need to cook that food, teaching them how to make a living in the city's restaurants and hotels.

Could there be a similarly creative way to help Haiti, I wondered? I happened to be nearby, in the Cayman Islands, when disaster struck. And I felt compelled to travel to Haiti to see if I could lend a hand.

Futurologists like to plan ahead for the world's biggest challenges, and there are few as daunting as the prospect of too many hungry people, with too few resources, competing for too little food. But you don't have to be a fortune-teller to see an apocalyptic future. You can fly two hours from Miami to begin to understand what our future might look like, and how we must begin to change course for ourselves and for our planet.

Because it was there in Haiti, amid what was still unbelievable suffering, that I could imagine a time – well before 2050 – when the brave people of this island could feed themselves with locally-grown food and cook their meals with clean energy. I could imagine a world where women would not have to waste their time and risk their lives to chop down precious wood; where young girls could go to school rather than search for cooking fuel; where families could breathe clean air in their homes, instead of the toxic fumes from the fire for their dinner. I could imagine a Haiti that no longer suffers from widespread deforestation because the people use charcoal to cook; where trees grow once again in healthy topsoil alongside local crops, and mudslides no longer threaten to kill people and destroy homes. I could imagine a time when the developed world could help the developing world – even in the middle of a humanitarian crisis – to adopt improved techniques of farming and cooking that would lead to a better future for us all.

In 1826 Jean Anthelme Brillat-Savarin, a great food philosopher, said, 'The future of nations will depend on how they feed themselves.' Almost two centuries after he wrote this line, the world faces both hunger and obesity. What can we do? The solution lies not just in food, but in how we farm, cook and handle food. Our biggest energy crisis isn't the price of gas. It's the way we cook and eat on a planet struggling to feed seven billion people. While it may seem strange to find the future in the midst of disaster, I found many answers in the rubble of Haiti.

For instance, we often do harm when we try to do good in a place like Haiti. To address the problem of hunger in Haiti, the US and so many other countries have tried to fix the problem by sending free food aid or selling heavily subsidized food. But this is a short-term solution that creates a long-term problem. Why? Because every grain of rice we send for free equals one less grain of rice that a farmer can sell in the market, or one less grain of rice that a farmer even bothers to plant. Food aid and agriculture subsidies are destroying the local economies and emptying the fields of developing countries. We can jump start the economy of a small country like Haiti, at the same time as feeding its population. The World Food Program claims that a significant percentage of aid is purchased in the countries it helps, but that was not my experience in Haiti. If our initial assistance harms farmers, we are doing more damage to an already struggling country.

Haiti depends on farming and exports just like other countries. But its farmers have the opposite problems of farmers in the USA. In America, a few big rich corporate farmers feed the poor with low quality food. At the same time, smaller, poorer farmers feed the rich with higher quality food. In Haiti, 70 per cent of the population is engaged in agriculture, but they produce less than 30 per cent of the national wealth. We cannot afford to use Haiti as a market for American food exports, to benefit wealthy American farmers. Haiti's farmers cannot compete with imported goods, which are often cheaper than their own.

Where they can compete – for instance, in growing mangoes for the US market – the industry association pays for compliance with the exhaustive standards of the US Department of Agriculture with all its permits, certifications and inspections. Colombian coffee makers have partnered with Nestle to help Haiti's farmers to manage the USDA process. But other smaller farmers cannot afford to sell their beans or peas to Europe or the USA. Instead of just throwing money into food aid, we should also think about helping Haiti to stand on its own by investing in the USDA process for other crops. That way we could bring jobs through farming to act as a catalyst for economic recovery.

Other solutions lie not in the future, but in the past. In 1810, Nicolas Appert published a book called *The Art of Preserving Animal and Vegetable Substances*. Appert's innovation was to preserve food safely in glass jars and bottles, paving the way for the canning industry. For many decades, canning was the only way to preserve foods and the method was embraced in Europe and America. Haiti, and other developing countries, could benefit enormously from returning to this old technique. Why? Because Haiti is a farming country, and preservation is a way to feed its own people when crop prices are low, and when times are tough. In the old days, canning was a low quality food source but today we have ways of making canned foods tasty.

So why don't we direct some of our international efforts into investments in a new food industry in Haiti? There are plenty of great NGOs doing wonderful work in the country, but the Haitian economy has hardly improved over many decades. I prefer the forward thinking of Dr Muhammad Yunus, the Nobel Peace Prize winner who saw that the poor could lift themselves up through microcredit. Yunus also developed a social business model, investing in jobs that filled a local need. That's what he did in Bangladesh with Danone, bringing calcium to children in the form of yoghurt, and also creating jobs through processing and distribution. It is a brilliant strategy, which could be adopted by NGOs. Yes, we need them to deliver basic services at times of chronic hunger. But they could also become the venture capitalists of food delivery in the same crisis-prone countries. Imagine Haitian women, near Fond Ferretes, who produce wonderfully ripe and tasty strawberries. With a little investment, they could improve their production, storage and delivery. They could have solar refrigeration, better boxes and branding, and a small delivery truck. They could have a phone messaging service to connect with customers or a sales person to sell more fruit. The old thinking was to give the cash to feed the hungry. The new thinking is to invest in mothers, so they can build a business to prosper, contribute to their communities and country, and improve food across the country – rather than importing food from far wealthier nations.

Just as important as how we farm is the question of how we cook. You and I only need a second or two to light up our stoves, or program the microwave. Seconds. Just seconds. We blink our eyes and we start cooking. Millions of people don't have that option.

For most of the world's population, cook stoves are the central energy challenge. We in the West prefer to think about the cost of oil and when we will exhaust our supplies of petroleum. Instead we need to concentrate on when we will exhaust our supplies of trees.

Charcoal is the main source of energy that Haitians use to cook. That is also the main reason why 98 per cent of the island is without trees, and why its young people develop so many respiratory illnesses. Dirty cook stoves are meant to feed families, but their smoke is killing people slowly and surely. Mothers hold their children in their arms as they cook, because they do not enjoy the first world luxury of a crib. The smoke they breathe is shortening their lives. It is also costing them precious time and money. Haitians spend up to 30 per cent of their daily income on fuel, and they often send their children to search for scraps of wood. They are searching on an island in a tropical climate where there are few trees left standing.

With no trees there is no food. With no trees, there are no roots to create and sustain a healthy soil. When the rainy season arrives, which should be a moment of joy and celebration of the life that water brings, the rain doesn't quench the dry soil. Instead it washes down the slopes of the mountains, creating erosion and often dangerous mudslides. Those waters become rivers, washing away the fertile soil, the home for seeds and food, washing away the homes of families, and sometimes, taking more human lives. This is an environmental nightmare from the simple desire to cook food.

Clean cook stoves can reduce such fuel usage by 70 per cent, freeing up money to buy food and education. Along the way, the children are free from hunting for wood and can go to school. The environment is free to recover with more trees, more topsoil and fewer mudslides. Such clean cook stoves are even being produced in Haiti today, with local labour. The challenge ahead of us is to make them both affordable and popular.

It is true that clean stoves are more expensive. But what if our international aid helped Haitians buy such clean stoves at a lower cost? We could save on the cost of future food aid, while Haitians save on the cost of food, fuel and their future. Along the way, we can also sustain new jobs in a struggling economy, producing the very clean stoves that will feed Haitians and restore their health. That's why the work of the Global Alliance For Clean Cook Stoves, led by the United Nations Foundation, is so important across the world.

The alliance – which I have joined as a culinary ambassador – has the simple but powerful idea to bring 100 million clean cooking stoves to 100 million households by the year 2020. When that happens, many girls won't have to climb a mountainside anymore. They can receive an education, and become productive members of society. They will not becomme ill from fumes. Their families will be able to buy books, clothing, and seeds to plant crops, with all the money saved from charcoal or wood. With good soil to farm, life is possible all around. By selling crops from the farm or the fruit of the trees, these families are creating wealth, empowering their communities, all through the power of food.

There are other solutions at hand today. At larger food centres, such as schools and hospitals, they can use pressure cookers heated by solar kitchens that concentrate the rays of the sun: a method I used myself on my first trip to Haiti in those first months after the devastating earthquake.

A cheaper and easier solution is to use natural gas, as they do in the Dominican Republic, on the other side of the island. Sadly Dominican trees along the border are illegally logged to turn into charcoal in Haiti. But gas is affordable, clean and readily available on both sides of the island. With a small investment by the international community, such as the World Bank or Inter-American Development Bank, Haiti could develop storage plants, distribution and tank supplies to help spread gas kitchens across the country. If our supremely wealthy energy companies want to give something back to this planet – something that will help the environment and some of the poorest people on Earth – they should channel their corporate donations into affordable gas supplies in countries like Haiti.

In Haiti, food is too easily seen as part of the seemingly unending crisis facing its people. It surely is one of their most pressing needs and the international community ought to help. By helping Haiti, we can build a safer, healthier, more prosperous future for food: from farming, to food companies, to cooking inside Haitian homes. If we can overcome the challenges facing Haiti after its earthquake, we can surely discover the food solutions for a planet facing such an uncertain future.

World Population Growth up till 2050 Occurs in Less Developed Countries

The expected human population growth from 1950 to 2050 for less developed and more developed countries shows that almost all expected growth is located in the poorer countries. This projection was presented by the United Nations in 2008. More developed regions are Australia, Canada, Europe, Japan, New Zealand and the United States. Less developed regions are all others. The United Nations also expect that over 90% of the population growth will take place in urban areas.

Data sources: United Nations, Department of Economic and Social Affairs, Population division, *World population prospects: the 2008 revision highlights* (New York: United Nations, 2009).

 Developing countries
Developed countries

World 1960
2,95 billion

World 1970
3,6 billion

World 1980
4,35 billion

World 1990
5,15 billion

World 2000
6 billion

World 2010
6,75 billion

World 2020
7,5 billion

World 2030
8,1 billion

World 2040
8,6 billion

World 2050
8,9 billion

The World's Future Water Use: A Global Increase in Irrigated Areas

FAO projections of the increase in areas that use irrigation in developed and developing countries towards 2050. The scenario presents a perspective on how the most important agricultural factors could evolve over time, without taking into account possible efforts to reduce poverty.

Source: J. Bruinsma (2009) 'The Resource Outlook to 2050: By How Much Do Land, Water Use and Crop Yields Need to Increase by 2050?', paper presented at the Expert Meeting on How to Feed the World in 2050, Food and Agriculture Organization of the United Nations, Rome.

Developing countries
Developed countries

World 1960
137 million ha

World 1970
170 million ha

World 1980
208 million ha

World 1990
244 million ha

World 2000
275 million ha

World 2010
290 million ha

World 2020
300 million ha

World 2030
308 million ha

World 2040
315 million ha

World 2050
320 million ha

Growth

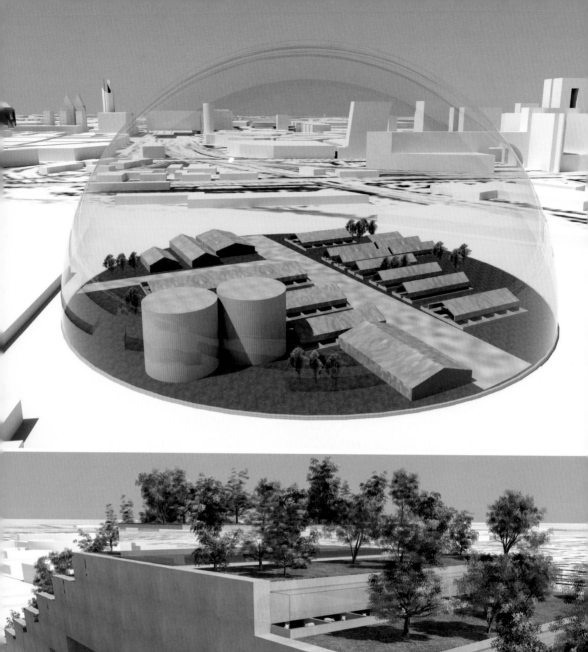

page 80 top and bottom

The Dutch architect Winy Maas and think tank The Why Factory designed an urban pig farm in the industrial area Binckhorst near the centre of The Hague in the Netherlands. The study envisioned a future where pigs would live in the vicinity of consumers, while the farms could deliver energy for the households nearby. See also p. 35.
Animation: The Snowball and The Bridge: Wieland & Gouwens, 2009.
Source: Winy Maas and The Why Factory.

page 81

An astronaut tends his hydroponic growth lab with vegetables on Mars. Crops of potatoes, soybeans, wheat, spinach, tomatoes, rice and herbs will provide the crews with added nutrition and variety. In the background a Mars lander.
Photo and source: NASA, Space Food Fact Sheets

page 82-83

In 1982 the American artist Agnes Denes created the iconic two-acre environmental artwork *Wheatfield - A Confrontation* in the middle of New York City. See also p. 33.
Photo and source: Agnes Denes, 1982.

page 84 top

The Australian eco design system coined 'permaculture' by Bill Morrison in 1982 seeks to benefit life in all its forms. Permablitz actions like the one in Melbourne not only transform backyards into edible gardens, but also build community networks. See also pp. 36, 90-96.
Photo and source: Adam Grubb

page 84 bottom

Pupils of Bancroft Elementary School and Kimball Elementary School help First Lady Michelle Obama with the harvest of vegetables in the garden of the White House. Michelle Obama's garden, the first in the White House since Eleanor Roosevelt's victory garden during World War II, educates children about locally grown produce in a country where obesity and diabetes have become national concerns.
Photo: Mark Wilson, 2009. Source: Getty Images

page 85

A worker with no previous agricultural experience harvests vegetables on one of the 21 hectares of compost-based vegetable gardens run by small cooperatives in and around the city of Caracas, Venezuela. In Cuba 300,000 people eat fresh fruit and vegetables from their urban and peri-urban gardens. 45 Cuban technicians have come to Caracas to educate the Venezuelans.
Photo: Giuseppi Bizzarri, 2004. Source: Food and Agriculture Organization

page 86 top

The Greenport Caofeidian Metropolitan Agro Industrial Park is a design for a food cluster situated near a Chinese metropolis that contains a variety of land- and season-independent production, processing, agrologistic and support functions. For many this kind of industrial ecology could be the way to global long-term food security.
Design & Layouts: Chen Pintan and Gao Chao, 2010. Source: Alterra, Wageningen University & Research

page 86-87 bottom

An inspiration collage showing potential for abundant use of fruit trees and berry bushes in The Hague, as part of Debra Solomon's project Foodscape Schilderswijk (2009-ongoing). See also p. 36.
Collage: Debra Solomon /Jaques Abelman, 2009. Source: culiblog.org

page. 87 top

Park Supermarkt by Dutch Van Bergen Kolpa Architects is a development model for a 1600 ha supermarket landscape in a conurbation in the Netherlands with a population of more than 7 million. See also p. 35.
Model: Werkplaats Vincent de Rijk, 2009. Source: Van Bergen Kolpa Architects and Vincent Kuypers (Alterra Wageningen UR)

page 88

A young Maasai woman with a cup of milk in the district of Morongoro, Tanzania. The livestock sector is one of the fastest growing parts of the agricultural economy, contributing 40% of the global value of agricultural production.
Photo: Giuseppe Bizzarri. Source: Food and Agriculture Organization in the series 'Towards a More Sustainable Livestock Sector'

Permaculture as a Permanent Culture

The Permaculturalist
Adam Grubb

When David Holmgren and Bill Mollison coined permaculture in Australia in the mid 70s as a counter movement to the industrial food system, no one imagined the global scale it would reach. Second generation permablitzer Adam Grubb from Melbourne introduces this more idle form of agriculture, which for many people has become a lifestyle.

Angelo Eliades doesn't eat a lot of vegetables, which is remarkable considering how many he grows in his inner suburban yard. He gives them away to friends and work colleagues. His eyes light up about the fruit though, and when I visited in the first week of the Melbourne summer we feasted on currants, various berries and the subtropical fruit babaco.

Angelo works full time as a technical writer but he looks absolutely in his element amongst the lush growth of his young garden. In 2008 he studied permaculture design and soon after he spent three months removing roses, building garden beds and completely making over his small yard. In the three years since, he has harvested (and carefully weighed) 14 kg of berries, 299 kg of other fruit, and 215 kg of veggies – which as it turns out, is more or less the amount of fruit and vegetables our government nutritionists recommend he should be eating. He refers to his garden, in permaculture parlance, as a 'food forest'. That might sound rather grandiose for a space of around 150m², less than half of which is covered with garden beds. Yet there are over 250 species of plants, around 80% of which are edible or medicinal. Most of the rest are 'support species': plants that provide ecosystem services such as soil building, capturing atmospheric nitrogen, producing strong fragrances to confuse pests, and attracting beneficial birds and insects with dense foliage or flowers. He claims not to have any pest problems, because there is a biological control for everything – well, everything except snails. 'For snails I need a blue-tongue lizard', he says, referring to an iconic native reptile, whose range unfortunately doesn't usually extend quite so far into the city.

The term permaculture was coined by Australians David Holmgren and Bill Mollison in the mid-1970s as a contraction of 'permanent agriculture' and later, as their scope and ambition grew, of 'permanent *culture*'. The initial idea, as expressed in *Permaculture One* (1978) was simple: the industrial food system is 'energy-expensive, mechanistic, and destructive of soil structure and quality', whereas peasant grain-based culture 'makes drudges of men, and . . . deserts of what once were forests'. A forest by comparison does well on its own terms without human labour, requires no inputs save air, sunshine and rain, and produces nothing we would understand as waste, unless you were to count oxygen.

They described a perennial agriculture of diverse plants and animals modelled on ecosystems, but composed largely of edible species, and species otherwise useful to humans (fuel, fibre and medicine). This approach, similar to many traditional systems of South East Asia and the Americas, promised a more idle form of agriculture, and one that restored, rather than depleted soils, biodiversity and other natural capital. Mollison, a charismatic academic and former shark fisherman and logger, took this vision of an edible Eden on the road, and it captured many imaginations in Australia, and soon globally.

Permaculture emerged amidst the 'back-to-the-landers' movement. However, much of the early experimentation took place in suburban yards. Angelo and myself are part of a growing global movement which is helping to bring ecologically designed food systems back to the city – not that, of course, they ever totally left.[1]

Mollison mixed an abrasive style and a kind of design genius with a tendency to think big, instigate, educate and, to be sure, exaggerate. Holmgren, a deeply thoughtful and less outgoing character, remained largely out of the public eye for almost 25 years, while he lived by and tested the theories on his own one hectare property in rural Victoria, while becoming one of the movement's deepest thinkers. Over the last 35 years, through the work of Mollison, Holmgren and many others, permaculture has come to represent far more than a system of forest gardening.

Even the *permanent* in permaculture has become something of a misnomer. The 1970s was an era of oil shocks and, just like many others, early permaculturists believed it was inevitable that fossil fuel consumption would begin to decline, taking much of consumer culture with it. The emphasis in permaculture is not on finding solutions for a future sustainable 'permanent' society, but rather for the period of transition, which might take generations.

After a two or three decade hiatus, concerns about energy and resource depletion have crept back into the fringes of public consciousness, however this time with a more authoritative voice. The International Energy Agency now concedes that conventional crude oil production peaked in 2006, the Chief Economist Fatih Birol warning, 'existing fields are declining so sharply that in order to stay where we are in terms of production levels, in the next 25 years we have to find and develop four new Saudi Arabias'.[2] Meanwhile, several international studies suggest that coal production may peak as soon as 2025[3], while the peak of natural gas production is tipped by the Association for the Study of Peak Oil and Gas to arrive around 2020.[4] I think it is reasonably clear that renewables and nuclear will not fill this energy gap in time and that the absolute peak in energy consumption is more or less upon us.

Author Richard Heinberg puts the predicament this way: 'Fossil fuels are the equivalent of a huge *inheritance* - one that we have spent quickly and not too wisely. Other energy sources will be more analogous to *wages*: we will have to work for what we get, and our spending will be restricted.'[5] Embarking on this transition we face some major challenges: a population of 7 billion and counting, an increasingly unstable climate, and severely depleted and damaged natural resources.

Permaculture co-originator David Holmgren coined a name for this era of decreasing energy use: 'energy descent'. In his book *Permaculture: Principles and Pathways Beyond Sustainability* (2002), he frames permaculture as a design system specifically for a post-peak society. Elsewhere he writes: 'permaculture is the wholehearted engagement with energy descent, as the opportunity for a world where less is better.'[6]

Due to the failure of international climate treaties, the political unpalatability of peak energy, and cascading financial crises, it is likely that much of the adaptive strategies will be piecemeal, reactive, local and decentralized. Permaculture thinking tends to emphasize the small and local scale, and ways in which individuals and communities can take immediate positive actions.

This permaculture is rather a broad design framework. It is tied together by ethical and design principles. There's perhaps no definitive set of principles since permaculturists tend to be an intractable bunch and like to rephrase and add their own flavour. However, all lists include similar themes and motifs: principles like 'Use and Value Diversity', 'Produce No Waste', 'Each Element Should Perform Many Functions', 'Use Small and Slow Solutions' and 'Use Edges and Value the Marginal'.[7/8] These principles are sometimes applied to finance and businesses, education, community governance, natural building, and other realms. Permaculture has become a broad umbrella under which strategies from all these areas are scrutinized, reshaped and networked. The global Transition Movement is a well-known example, a kind of community-driven regional planning framework to help towns and regions prepare themselves for energy descent.

Despite its rather nebulous scope, much permaculture design is indeed practiced in home gardens. In my city of Melbourne and elsewhere, groups of permaculture enthusiasts (myself and Angelo included) facilitate open-to-the-public garden makeover days called permablitzes. Anywhere from 15 to 100 people may book in, and with an explosion of their energy, free workshops and shared food, a garden gets transformed into an edible landscape over the course of a day, based on a permaculture design. Everyone learns and has a good time.

Permaculture design cannot be prescriptive, and must always start with assessing the motivations, skills, resources, tastes and desires of the people involved. We then consider the landscape – observing soil, slope, water harvesting potential, sun and wind exposure.

Many of the strategies we employ are common sense, or at least seem like they should be. We like to place high-maintenance features like veggie gardens where they are most easily seen and accessed, ideally right outside the kitchen door. Lower maintenance systems like edible forest gardens often suit front yards, fence lines, or less visited areas. We try to place all elements in micro-climates that optimally suit them. For instance in Melbourne veggies benefit from full winter sun and afternoon summer shade. Deciduous trees and vines can provide summer shade to buildings and veggies. We aim to match the outputs of one design element with the needs of another, and to create synergies. Chickens for example provide fertilizer, weed and pest control for fruit trees, while the fruit trees provide shade and fallen fruit for the chickens. There are more levels than I can do justice to here, and yet it's not so complicated either.

For most permablitz hosts and my professional clients, gardening is something of a lifestyle choice. Yet many of the principles and strategies have been stress-tested and developed in more vulnerable situations like Uganda, post-tsunami Aceh, and post-independence East Timor. Permaculture practitioners were influential in Cuba in the 1990s as the country made the incredibly challenging transition to low input agriculture following the collapse of the Soviet Union, taking with it Cuba's access to subsidized oil and fertilizers.[9] Havana now produces for all of the fresh produce needs of its inhabitants in urban and peri-urban gardens.[10]

It may be under pressures closer to these scenarios that the denizens of Melbourne and other cities in 2050 employ their food growing strategies. However, it's not possible that cities could ever be completely self-sufficient – their very existence depends on storable, transportable and concentrated agricultural surpluses. Like Havana, they may produce all of their own fruit and vegetables, but it would be an impressive effort to produce more than 10% of their citizens' required calories in temperate climates – that's what Angelo produces in his yard (along with around 30% of his vitamin and mineral requirements).

Grains, potatoes and other high-carbohydrate crops will need to be mainly grown on farms. Agriculture is already struggling under the increasing pressures of a destabilized climate and high energy costs. More organic, lower-input and labour-intensive farms will likely prove more resilient as these trends continue, as small-scale organic output per acre today is already higher than that of non-organic farms. Given these factors, the centuries-long process of urbanization may begin to run in reverse, even as the city itself takes on more of an agricultural flavour.

While the city will not be self-sufficient, more food production within it will bring many benefits equal to those of the food value alone. Remarkably, exposure to foliage improves one's sense of wellbeing, attention span, intelligence, and impulse control,[11/12] while gardening offers gentle exercise and can be an even more therapeutic process. More fresh food is associated with better nutrition, including more vitamins, minerals, antioxidants, omega-3 fatty acids, and thus anti-aging, greater fitness, and again greater attention spans, impulse control and even fewer violent crimes(!)[13/14]

The excess of nutrients travelling through cities currently creates pollution problems, including methane emissions from landfill and sewerage. These nutrients can be caught through composting to create highly productive urban soils. With more growing spaces and water storage, the entire hydrology of the urban region and the health of its waterways and fisheries can improve. The urban heat island effect is reduced, while, as mentioned, strategically placed deciduous vines and fruit trees can be used to lower heating and cooling costs for buildings. Around one third of Australian households' greenhouse emissions can be traced to the food system.

Growing food right outside the back door using organic strategies has radically less greenhouse impact, most obviously in terms of food miles.

At the social level, the sharing of gardening strategies and crop cultivars can help build connections across neighbourhood fences, and across cultures. Both increased self-reliance and stronger community connections lead to greater resilience in times of crisis. At the political level these same two factors, and the literal grounded-ness that comes from gardening, might subtly – and I don't think this is an exaggeration – make people more resistant to fear-based politics, something that may raise its ugly head higher in unstable times.

I once heard the late economist David Fleming say something to the effect that, 'localization stands, at best, at the fringes of political possibility. Yet it has in its favour the decisive factor that there will be no alternative'. It's a worthy task then to 'run down the slope' of energy descent a little faster than others, to set up viable and replicable models for the future of a more localized, resilient, and self-reliant city.

The permaculture framework comes with its share of historical baggage and idiosyncrasies. But for all that, it may just represent the best existing set of principles for navigating this era of energy descent. Insofar as that judgement is correct, then the more it is used, the more abundant our lives shall be.

Feeding the World:
A New Paradigm for 2050

The Industrialist
Stephan Tanda

Austrian-born Stephan Tanda, member of the managing board of Royal DSM Inc., which operates on global markets such as food and dietary supplements, pharmaceuticals, alternative energy and bio-based materials, introduces a new type of company that is driven by the notion of shared value in the fight against the global food crises.

Our world is facing a daunting combination of mega trends – population growth, climate change, resource scarcity and urbanization among them – that conspire to challenge our basic ability to provide people with enough food and nutrition to survive, prosper, and live healthy, and increasingly longer lives.

At first sight, the prognosis is bleak. Population growth and rising standards of living are placing unprecedented levels of pressure on arable land, which is already diminishing. At the same time, minerals and raw materials that are essential for maintaining agricultural productivity are becoming depleted at such a rate that some scientists now talk about Peak Phosphate as a threat to the food supply, much in the same way as Peak Oil is threatening our energy supply.

Already today's food crisis is so bad, that almost one billion people – one in seven of us – suffer from a lack of food and more than two billion suffer from malnutrition, not getting the essential micronutrients such as vitamins and minerals. And the problem is not restricted to the developing world where calories might be scarce, but it affects the industrialized world too, where large sections of the population lack essential micronutrients in their diet, which are vital to maintaining good health.

Are there solutions in sight? There are certainly some fine minds from governments, NGOs, academia and the private sector now concentrating on the problems. At DSM, we have deep roots in health and nutrition and are committed to using our science to create brighter lives. We believe that creating shared value, and helping to address these societal challenges, is nothing less than vital to our future success.

This is largely because our corporate philosophy is to judge ourselves by how well we address the global trends that impact our customers and stakeholders: shifts in population; health and wellness; climate and energy, and we have a strong belief that we can play a role in bringing about sustainable solutions. To address the food crisis, for example, we are convinced that a focus on proper nutrition is absolutely critical, in addition to increasing the sheer volume of food production. In fact the focus on nutrition is an essential new paradigm to feed the world sustainably.

Tackling Hidden Hunger in the Developing World

Including nutrition in our quest for lasting answers to the food crisis is in a sense widening the scale of the problem. We need to grow, stay healthy, make a positive economic contribution, and break the cycle of poverty and ill health.

This 'hidden hunger' problem represents a crippling burden on the world, and that's before taking into account population growth, the strain on natural resources, and climate change. Therefore addressing it now is vital. The World Bank has calculated that hidden hunger can reduce a country's GDP by as much as 3%. Collectively, vitamin and mineral deficiencies account for an estimated 7,3% of the global disease burden, with iron, vitamin A and zinc deficiencies all ranking among the top ten leading causes of death due to disease in developing countries.

Perhaps most damning of all, micronutrient deficiencies are leading to widespread health problems globally, impairing the mental development of 40-60% of infants in the developing world, debilitating the health of half a million women and leading to over 60,000 deaths during childbirth every year.

Getting nutrition right, then, would have a much bigger positive impact on the health and wellbeing of our population than merely ensuring that everyone gets enough calories to survive. It's why the Copenhagen Consensus of leading economists determined that addressing malnutrition is the single most cost effective development intervention we can make in addressing a key global problem, with 17 dollars returned for every dollar invested.

At DSM, we have worked hard to gain a better understanding of the scope of this problem and how we as an organization can use our leading position as a producer of vitamins, enzymes, nutritional lipids and other nutritional ingredients to address these acute needs outside the usual markets we serve. Through long-running collaborations with humanitarian organizations such as Sight and Life and Vitamin Angels, we now have a much clearer idea when and where micronutrient deficiencies are most pronounced[1] and where to concentrate resources to defeat them.

Mapping out the problem also gives us a much better idea where to focus our global nutrition research agenda. For example, in helping us develop MixMe™, small sachets of micronutrients that cost only a few dollars per person per year and can be added to any food dish, or NutriRice™, fortified kernels enriched with vitamins and minerals that look, taste and cook exactly like ordinary rice. Both have proven to be very effective to help alleviate malnutrition.

People often talk about sustainability narrowly in terms of the environment, but nutrition needs to be sustainable too. We are committed to supporting emergency relief efforts. At the same time we recognize that nutrition aid alone is not a long-term answer. Which is why we are involved to build capability and capacity at the local level through collaborations and key partnerships, such as the UN World Food Programme (WFP), the Scaling Up Nutrition (SUN) initiative, the Global Alliance for Improved Nutrition (GAIN), and Partners in Food Solutions, putting in place supply chains and distribution models that will allow communities and local farmers to take control of their own destiny.

Key in DSM's partnerships are the employee volunteer programs. DSM employees have been working on projects in countries like Zambia, Kenya, Nepal and Bangladesh with local communities and manufacturers to transfer knowledge and help them build, evaluate and refine their business models and logistical infrastructure in order to ensure they are better equipped to deliver and benefit from enhanced nutrition. Crucially, this is about developing local capacity that is sustainable.

This approach to sustainable nutrition enables agencies like the WFP to concentrate its resources where they are needed most, helping people in disaster zones, while acting as a catalyst for local economic development, which creates local markets, jobs, and better infrastructure.

The Role of Nutrition in Advanced Societies

The health impacts of micronutrient deficiencies are not limited to the developing world. In the developed world, our ageing population and changing lifestyles and dietary habits lead to dramatic increases of non-communicable diseases (NCDs) such as cancer, obesity, diabetes and heart disease, which drive a massive rise in the cost of health care. Long term health, including a reduction of these diseases, can be positively impacted by nutrition.

In fact, the dramatically increasing NCDs collectively kill 36 million people every year, making them the world's biggest killer. In the developed world, they account for 30% of healthcare budgets. The problem is growing with such ferocity that in 2011 the UN convened a special summit to come up with new ways to tackle them and reverse the chilling trend; this is only the second time in its history that a health issue has been discussed at a UN General Assembly.

Lifestyle is often to blame for this epidemic, and governments today are learning that the onset of NCDs can be at least ameliorated and at best tackled head on by better nutrition. All of the top six killer NCDs are linked to diet, which means that not only can better nutrition save billions in health care costs, it can also lead to a better quality of life over the course of a lifetime and greater economic participation.

A great example here is vitamin D, which can reduce the risk of osteoporosis, falls and fractures by 20%. Osteoporosis leads to over 9 million fractures worldwide every year and costs European health care services 25 billion per year, making it a major, if low-profile, public health problem. By working with the International Osteoporosis Foundation, we are now beginning to get a much better idea of the scale of the problem, and how to ensure people get their required intake levels through the right combination of sunlight exposure, diet, and fortification and supplementation solutions. We also know how cost-effective it can be – with research in Germany alone showing it can deliver health care cost savings in the region of 600 to 800 million euro per year.

Thanks to dynamic strides in nutrition science, we now realize that nutrition gives healthcare policymakers an amazing tool to improve people's health and quality of life and manage the disease burden that comes with ageing populations. A holistic, full life cycle approach is needed to make sure this is capitalized on, starting with promoting good nutrition from conception onwards, meeting the needs of pregnant mothers, and continuing into the first thousand days of a child's life, where recent research tells us that a poor diet will programme the body for health problems into adulthood and later life.

Towards a Holistic Solution for Solving our Food, Nutrition, Material and Energy Needs

There is no doubt that most diets do not provide enough of the right micronutrients and that micronutrient fortification and supplementation strategies have a major role to play in the new paradigm of nutrition and preventive health. This should be a priority for policymakers, health professionals, businesses and consumers today and a centrepiece of global strategy for feeding the world as we move towards 2050 and beyond.

But to ensure such a strategy's success, the issue of food and nutrition needs to be seen through the prism of our changing world. With fossil fuels running out, biomass is increasingly being used to fulfil some of our non-food needs as well, such as materials and energy production.

At DSM, we take a holistic approach to help solve some of the world's great challenges: there is no point solving one problem if it exacerbates another. Which is why, drawing on our hundred-year history of fermentation and knowledge of both materials and life sciences, we have identified technologies that focus on converting the non-edible parts of plants, such as cellulose and lignin, to meet our non-food needs.

For instance, converting biomass that is derived either from agricultural residue, such as corn stover, bagasse, or from specific crops that can be grown on marginal land that is unsuitable for food production. It is critical that this technology is allowed to establish itself, as with the right kinds of protection for land use and an appropriate framework to protect biodiversity, water supplies and other critical human rights, it will help us find an answer to both our food and our non-food needs in a sustainable way.

Used correctly, biomass' potential actually goes beyond protecting land for food production and helping solve our non-food needs: it can actually help us produce both. It's an exciting prospect with potentially massive implications for our future food supply. Here's how it could work: bio refineries produce protein as a side stream from the refining process. Today, this protein is extracted at the end of the refining process, by which time it is in bad shape and only fit for animal feed. At DSM, we are working on ways to extract the protein earlier in the refining process and find ways to improve the quality so that the organic protein is fit for human consumption.

This new source of organic protein could, in part, replace animal protein. If successful, we could contribute to another one of the major challenges: how to manage the exponential growth in demand for animal protein. On the other hand we invest heavily in making the production of animal protein more and more efficient and sustainable, for example through the use of feed enzymes.

I believe we are at a turning point in the quest to build a sustainable future for our world. There has been a welcome recognition among key stakeholders, Hilary Clinton and Ban Ki-moon among them, of the powerful role nutrition can play in improving the health, livelihood and potential of the poor and undernourished. At the same time, the private sector is coming to be recognized as an equal partner, and for its part is stepping up and delivering creative solutions to ease the burden of disease and give hope to millions.

In the bio-economy, giant leaps of progress are being made, and already in 2013 the first large-scale second generation bio refineries converting cellulose will start to operate.

Maintaining this trajectory requires a new type of company focused on the creation of 'shared value' that benefits society, the planet and individuals as well as investors.

At its most basic level the concept of shared value rejects the assumption that there is a trade-off between business and economic benefit on the one hand, and societal and environmental needs on the other. Rather, shared value is premised on the recognition that it is only by really addressing the needs and challenges of society that value is created for shareholders. The outcome of shared value is by definition beneficial to all stakeholders, although the relative balance between these stake-holders is driven by a wide range of factors and variables.

In this way, our customers derive value by being able to offer end users improved products; communities and the planet derive value from the impact of more sustainable, long-lasting, safer, healthier and more nutritious alternatives. This is our vision at DSM: we call it Bright Science. Brighter Living.

Land per Person: A Reduction Towards 2050

FAO projections of the amount of available arable land in developed and developing countries up till 2050. The scenario presents a perspective on how the most important agricultural factors evolve over time, without taking into account possible efforts to reduce poverty. Note that the negative impact of the reduction in available land may be diminished by increased yields.

Source: J. Bruinsma (2009) 'The Resource Outlook to 2050: By How Much Do Land, Water Use and Crop Yields Need to Increase by 2050?', paper presented at the Expert Meeting on How to Feed the World in 2050, Food and Agriculture Organization of the United Nations, Rome.

○ **Developed countries**
● **Developing countries**

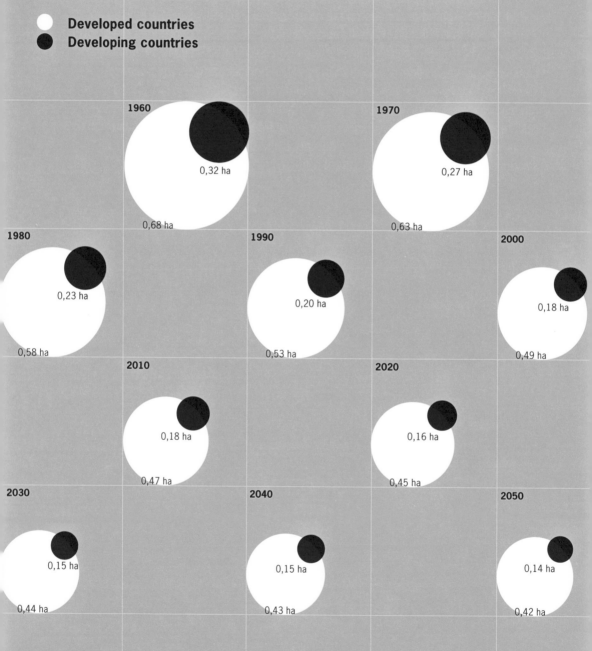

1960 — 0,32 ha — 0,68 ha

1970 — 0,27 ha — 0,63 ha

1980 — 0,23 ha — 0,58 ha

1990 — 0,20 ha — 0,53 ha

2000 — 0,18 ha — 0,49 ha

2010 — 0,18 ha — 0,47 ha

2020 — 0,16 ha — 0,45 ha

2030 — 0,15 ha — 0,44 ha

2040 — 0,15 ha — 0,43 ha

2050 — 0,14 ha — 0,42 ha

Water Footprint per Product: Animal Products Demand Most Water

Global average amount of water (in litres) needed to produce one kilo of the products listed in 2008.
Note that strong variations occur depending on the method of production.

Source: A.Y. Hoekstra, A.K., Chapagain, *Globalization of water: sharing the planet's freshwater resources* (Oxford: Blackwell Publishing, 2008)

Crop

Rice	**Groundnuts (in shell)**	**Wheat**	**Maize**	**Apple or pear**
3400 liter/kg	3100 liter/kg	1300 liter/kg	900 liter/kg	700 liter/kg

Orange	**Potato**	**Cabbage**	**Tomato**	**Lettuce**
460 liter/kg	250 liter/kg	200 liter/kg	180 liter/kg	130 liter/kg

Animal product

Bovine leather	**Beef**	**Sheep**	**Cheese**	**Pork**
16,600 liter/kg	15,500 liter/kg	6100 liter/kg	5000 liter/kg	4800 liter/kg

Milk powder	**Goat**	**Chicken**	**Egg**	**Milk**
4600 liter/kg	4000 liter/kg	3900 liter/kg	3300 liter/kg	1000 liter/kg

Harvest and Process

page 105

Women farmers put beans in sacks in eastern Sri Lanka. The FAO-project will enable the 20,000 returning farming households to restart the production of vegetables, fruit and poultry.

Photo: Ishara Kodikara, 2010. Source: Food and Agriculture Organization in the project 'Enhancing food security and nutrition among the most vulnerable farm families in eastern Sri Lanka'

page 106-107

Set net fishermen trap salmon when the fish swim close to shore in Bristol Bay, Alaska. This kind of fishing is a seasonal operation run by local families, who also work at other jobs to supplement their income.

Photo: Michael Melford, 2009. Source: National Geographic/Getty Images

page 108 top

Industrial fishing nets in sunset.

Photo: Rechitan Sorin. Source: Shutterstock

page 108 bottom

Wheat Harvest Combine in Wala Wala, Washington, United States

Photo: Anthony Boccaccio. Source: Getty Images

page 109

in 2010 98% of the cassava harvest in Thailand was exported to China for biofuel. The increasing use of crops for biofuel is contributing to soaring food prices, and in their wake food riots and political turmoil in Algeria, Egypt and Bangladesh.

Photo: Agnes Dherbeys. Source: The New York Times, April 6, 2011

page 110-111

Salt workers from the Afar tribe in the Danakil desert in Ethiopia, one of the hottest places on Earth.

Photo: Pascal Boegli, 2008. Source: pbOOg.cOm

page 112 top

A woman working in one of the 66 chicken processing plants in North Carolina, US. The approximately 2,500 workers process more than 400,000 chickens a day. In this economically depressed area there are few other job opportunities.

Photo: Glow Images, 2007. Source: Hollandse Hoogte

page 112 bottom

In this German slaughterhouse the pig's haunches are carved into smaller pieces on the assembly line.

Photo: J.S. Peifer. Source: Reporters/AP

page 113

The German artist Christian Jankowski, who once roasted a piece of the skin of his toe to see what it tastes like, made a series of art works called The Angels of Revenge, an investigation of the horror film genre. The act of cannibalism may be repulsive, but there is an attraction to that repulsion, according to the artist.

Photo: Christian Jankowski, 2006. Source: Lisson Gallery

page 114-115

A technician takes a sample from one of the incubation tanks in a yoghurt plant.

Photo: Maximilian Stock Ltd. Source: Getty Images

page 116

Workers on a Delmonte banana plant in the northeast of Costa Rica throw the bananas into a chemical solution before shipping them off to the United States. Bananas are one of the biggest export products of Costa Rica.

Photo and source: Yvonne Wassink, 2005

page 117 top

Woman processing cookies in a market stall in Tokyo, Japan.

Photo and source: Yvonne Wassink, 2006

page 117 bottom

Processing and packing of tuna fish into tins at a French-owned, international company in the Antsiranana harbour in the northern prefecture of Madagascar.

Photo: H. Wagner. Source: Food and Agriculture Organization in the series 'The Whole World Will Profit'

page 118 top and bottom + page 119

The Arctic Food Network designed by architects and urban planners Lola Sheppard and Mason White of the Canadian Lateral Office seeks to develop a model to enhance the economic and cultural infrastructure of the Inuit community, who are now dependent on expensive processed food products imported from the south. See also pp. 192-1997.

Render and source: Lateral Office

page 120

Food on space shuttles has improved since the first flight to the moon. Where John Glenn found the menu somewhat limited, and other astronauts had to endure freeze-dried powders and semi-liquids squeezed out of tubes, contemporary space travelers eat thermostabilized fish and fruits and ready-to-eat nuts, granola bars and cookies. Flour tortillas seem to be the favorite bread item of shuttle astronauts because they don't have crumbs that foul the instruments.

Photo and source: NASA, Space Food Fact Sheets

A Tale of Two Hungry Cities

The Rural Sociologist
Johannes S.C. Wiskerke

The Dutch agronomist Johannes Wiskerke, Chair of the
Rural Sociology Group of Wageningen University and
Research Centre in the Netherlands goes sci-fi and jumps
to the year 2050, when the two prevailing paradigms in
agriculture have created completely different societies.

On Friday morning 20th May 2050 Pichelle O'Mollan, the mayor of San Acivitas, has breakfast with her children when her mobile device informs her that the world's population has just hit 9 billion. This is just 10 months after another historical demographic milestone, namely that of an urban population tripling the rural population. That same moment the mayor of Maleurbe, Peter Threws Jr, also receives this information from his advisor Dunga Denha, when she enters his office with several pre-packed bread rolls for their lunch meeting. The news about this demographic milestone makes both mayors reminiscent of previous milestones in the development of the world's population: in May 2007 for the first time in history more people were living in urban than in rural areas and about four and a half years later the 7th billion person was welcomed to the planet.

Back in those days, the world was facing a series of food scares and crises. This began in the 1990s with outbreaks of BSE, classical swine fever and foot-and-mouth disease. This was complemented simultaneously with several food safety scandals such as dioxin contamination of animal feed, salmonella contamination of poultry and melamine contamination of milk powder. In 2008 world food prices increased dramatically, creating a global crisis and causing political, social and economic instability in both poor and developed nations. The rapid increase in food prices re-occurred in 2010, creating further political instability, leading, for instance, to the fall of the Tunisian government, which in turn triggered the collapse of long-lasting dictatorial regimes in Egypt and Libya.

At that time most experts were of the opinion that the combination of rising oil prices, increasing demand for biofuels, export restrictions and crop shortfalls from natural disasters were the main causes of the food price hikes. They therefore proposed to spatially cluster agricultural functions by bringing together high-productive plant-based and animal-based production and processing along industrial lines, combined with the closing of water and nutrients cycles. 'Double the world's food production while reducing the environmental impact' became a much celebrated slogan with agroparks as its symbolic manifestation.

A few experts, however, came to a different conclusion and stated that the 2008 food crisis was not an extraordinary event, but a sign of a failing food system. They argued that the fundamentals underneath the food system had changed drastically since the beginning of the 20th century, when agricultural policy focused on increasing production to eradicate hunger. Since then, the relationship between people, food systems and the planet had been completely restructured. They therefore argued that new policies were needed to address the core issues within the dominant food system – climate change, water, biodiversity, energy, population growth, waste, land, soil, labour, dietary change and public health – simultaneously and systemically in order to meet the goals of sustainability, equity and health.

The Tale of Maleurbe

'Which of these bread rolls would you like, Mr. Mayor?' Dunga asks.

'Aren't there any with smoked salmon?' Peter asks. 'You know I love it and it's produced and processed right here in Maleurbe's agropark RURA.'

'That's true, Mr. Mayor,' Dunga replies, 'but in the Esuriit metropolitan area, 4500 miles up north, there is an enormous demand for salmon. Apparently the human nutrition expert of the Lorem Scientia University in Carordinata, Professor Francois Coquere, has discovered that the new salmon variety developed in the RURA lab has certain anti-carcinogenic features. The majority of the Esuriitians is obsessed with health, so if there is scientific evidence that a food product has health benefits they are willing to pay much more than the usual price. So now RURA is selling all its salmon to consumers in Esuriit. This implies that we'll have to do without for the time being.'

'So much for my father's local-for-local idea.' Peter sighs.

'Your father's what?' Dunga asks.

Peter begins to explain: 'Back in 2012 my father, Peter Threws Sr, was head of Maleurbe's planning department. At that time Maleurbe was facing food riots due to rapidly rising food prices and shortages of basic commodities. As Maleurbe's population was growing fast and more food riots were expected, my father came to the conclusion that drastic measures had to be taken to improve food security. He was very inspired by the agropark-concept. He was convinced that agroparks held the promise to avoid future food riots as the basic aim was to produce all basic food stuffs at low prices in a metropolitan region for the inhabitants of that region, hence local-for-local. So he developed a master plan to modernize Maleurbe. This included the development of new residential areas for people living in impoverished neighbour-hoods, the conversion of these neighbourhoods into agroparks and recreational parks and improvement of the transport infrastructure. Part of his plan was also to get rid of all the food growing plots in the impoverished areas.'

'Why?' Dunga asks.

'For several reasons.' Peter answers. 'First of all the small amounts of food produced on these plots did not contribute significantly to urban food security. Second, because of food safety concerns, as these food products were not inspected. Finally, the spatial intertwinement of small-scale food production and living was nothing but visual pollution. To modernize Maleurbe, the planning department adhered to a strict zoning philosophy: residential areas with gardens only allowed to have an aesthetic function, parks inside the city for recreational use, agroparks for food production, rural production areas for the production of animal feed and staple crops and the rest of the countryside for nature and recreation.'

'But what about our agroparks?' Dunga aks. 'They produce all the basic foodstuffs plus a whole range of other products in quantities sufficient to feed the city, but I sense that you have doubts about it.'

'The fact that there is no salmon available for Maleurbe just because consumers elsewhere are able to pay more, shows that local-for-local isn't guaranteed.' Peter explains.

'But salmon is a luxury product.' Dunga replies.

'That's true,' Peter responds, 'but we've had periods in the past when we were even short of vegetables, simply because there was an enormous foreign demand for flowers, so most of the vegetable production space was converted into flower production space.'

'But can't we oblige the agroparks to first supply the consumers of our city with all basic food stuffs and only export surpluses?' Dunga asks.

'No, we can't.' Peter answers. 'The agroparks are owned by transnational corporations and banks. They invested heavily in the development of the agroparks and therefore they decide what and how much is produced and to whom products are sold. I begin to see that removing food entirely from the public realm is an inherent design fault of agroparks.'

'Any other faults?' Dunga inquires.

'Yes, unemployment and poverty.' Peter replies. 'Before the agroparks were built, many food products were produced on small-scale family farms in the countryside surrounding Maleurbe. Working conditions on these farms were harsh and agropark-proponents proclaimed that modern societies should no longer accept this. In agroparks the entire production chain would be automated, so by relocating food production from small-scale family farms to agroparks these harsh working conditions could be eradicated. However, one crucial aspect was totally overlooked. There was no other economic sector at that time growing at a rate that enabled it to absorb those discarded by the modernization of food production, so many people became unemployed.'

'So what can we do to reduce the vulnerability of our food system?' Dunga asks.

'There is someone I could ask for advice.' Peter responds. 'I'll give her a call.'

The Tale of San Acivitas

'Mum, what's on your mind?' Pichelle's son asks.

'Well Isaac', she says, 'the news about the 9 billion people milestone made me think of your grandmother.'

'Why does grandma come to mind?' her daughter asks.

Pichelle smiles and replies: 'I can understand that this seems odd to you, Sasha, but let me explain. In 2012 San Acivitas was growing fast and facing challenges regarding socioeconomic inequalities, public health and quality of the living environment. Life expectancy of people living in impoverished neighbourhoods was approximately ten years less than that of the rest of the city's population, mainly because the share of overweight was highest in these poor neighbourhoods. We then spoke of food deserts.'

'What's a food desert?' Isaac asks. 'And why were mainly poor people fat?'

'Food deserts were urban areas where it was difficult to have access to healthy, affordable food and they were most common in low-socioeconomic minority communities.' Pichelle responds. 'So they were not neighbourhoods without food outlets but neighbourhoods without grocery stores, supermarkets and fresh food markets yet with mini-marts and fast food establishments. And back in 2012 fast food and processed food products were much cheaper than fresh food.'

'What a strange world back then,' Sasha says, 'but you still haven't made clear to us what this has to do with grandma'.

'Well, in 2008 your grandma completed her PhD research on the causes of health inequalities. She concluded that differences in people's diets were a major cause of health inequalities.'

'That sounds pretty obvious.' Sasha interrupts.

'You're right', Pichelle continues, 'but her study also revealed that differences in diets, and thus health inequalities, were strongly influenced by the food environment. For instance, people living in neighbourhoods with easy access to fresh food markets had a better health status than people living in food deserts. And the more community gardens in a neighbourhood, the better the health status of its residents. But also children attending schools that served healthy school meals and that offered special food and farm-to-school programmes were healthier and had less overweight compared to other children.'

'So what did grandma recommend on the basis of her study?' Isaac asks.

'Basically she called upon the municipality to develop an integrated food policy', Pichelle answers, 'or, as she used to say, a policy that would connect the dots between food, health, social justice, environment, education and land use. The difficulty at that time was that food was not considered to be an urban issue and that eating healthy or unhealthy was considered to be your own responsibility in which the municipality should not intervene. However, she did find several like-minded persons, from diverse professional and social backgrounds, with whom she founded the San Acivitas food policy council. They developed an action plan that initially focused on four key themes: eradication of hunger by providing inexpensive nutritious food to low socioeconomic communities, reducing diet-related diseases by creating a better food environment, preserving land for food production in and near the city, and developing new forms of urban food production such as edible balconies, productive green roof-tops and in-door hydroponics.'

'Was the food policy council able to make a difference?' Sasha inquires.

'Yes and no.' Pichelle replies. 'Yes, because more and more people started to talk about and understand the importance of healthy and sustainable food for the city. No, because it was not an official advisory body for the city council and thus could not really influence political decision making. This all changed when Marion Recubo was elected as mayor in 2012. She changed the status of the food policy council; all municipal plans and proposed policies were evaluated by the food policy council with regard to their expected social, economic and ecological impact on the metropolitan food system. So when a plan for building a new shopping centre had to be assessed, the council would for instance only approve the plan if it included the possibility for rooftop food production, could be easily reached by public transport and would accommodate a fresh food market. To give the political and legislative support to the key action themes of the food policy council, Marion asked my mother to set up and lead the new Department of Food, Health & Community Development.'

'And did she do a good job?' Isaac asks.

'Oh yes, she did!' Pichelle proudly proclaims. 'The fact that the two of you didn't know what a food desert is, that you couldn't see the link between poverty and obesity and that you find it strange that fresh food used to be more expensive than processed food already shows how much has changed. Furthermore, in San Acivitas obesity rates have been reduced substantially, everyone has access to healthy food, socio-economic differences in life expectancy have almost vanished, and most of our food is grown on farms, rooftops and indoor production units in and around the city. And by giving high priority to productive green in the city the urban microclimate has improved substantially.'

Around the time Pichelle's mother had completed her PhD thesis, her parents got divorced. Both her parents were very committed to the challenge of urban food security, but always disagreed about the way to achieve that. A crucial event that ended their marriage in 2008 was a short movie about Greenport Shanghai, a then futuristic animation of an envisaged agropark in Shanghai. Pichelle's father was convinced he had just witnessed the solution to urban food security. Her mother, on the other hand, had just seen a horror scenario, i.e. the final step in complete corporate food control. Her solution to improve the quality of the urban foodscape was seen as totally unrealistic by Pichelle's father. After the divorce he moved to another city, remarried and had a son.

Pichelle's phone rings. Her display informs her that it is her half-brother Peter, who has recently also become mayor. 'Hi sis, I need some food advice', she hears him say.

We Want Food, Entertainment and Art . . .

The Architect / Urbanist
Jorge Mario Jáuregui

The act of eating as a social and cultural phenomenon that unites the less privileged inhabitants of the favelas of Rio de Janeiro with the more privileged residents in the rest of the city is the starting point of a tour of the favela with the Brazilian architect and planner Jorge Mario Jáuregui. Brazil's famous bean stew with trimmings, *feijoada completa*, has no fixed recipe, just like Jáuregui's approach to urban design.

Feijoada completa (Bean stew with all the trimmings)

'Hey girl, you're gonna like this!
I've invited some guys over to hang out.
They're so hungry they can't begin to tell me.
They've been thirsty since the day before yesterday.
So lay in enough ice-cold beer for a battalion
And let's put on some water for those beans!'

Chico Buarque

The act of eating has historically revolved around the need to feed ourselves, but at the same time it is a social and cultural phenomenon.

Today's megacities are places where all kinds of ideals can find expression, and where luxury and poverty – excess of food on the one hand and hunger on the other – reflect the sombre side of humanity that Sigmund Freud termed 'civilization and its discontents'. Food is not just about the way we eat but also about the way we live and relate to others, which now needs to be redefined in terms of an existential ecology.

Logic, intelligence and solidarity are incompatible with present-day humanity as it reaches the threshold of seven billion human beings, some of whom are suffering from excess of things and others from lack of them, both of which show just how necessary it is to reorient our behaviour and habits in terms of what the philosopher Thierry Paquot calls 'existential ecology', i.e. modifying both individual and collective behaviour. Obviously this calls for social intelligence, for there is an answer to every problem – all we need are new, democratic forms of organization and representation, within each country as well as at an international, global level in the bodies that represent the various countries of the world.

The chaotic processes of present-day urbanization include aspects that are physical (infrastructural, urbanistic, environmental), social (economic, cultural, existential) and ecological (mental ecology, social ecology, environmental ecology), aspects of public safety and their interactions with contemporary issues relating to changes in labour relations, communications, use of cities and eating habits.

Calls to articulate the divided city and society thus cover numerous aspects of citizenship. Today, as police forces are set up in Rio de Janeiro's main *favelas* (shanty towns) and urban development is fostered by Brazil's Growth Acceleration Programme, new ways of access are being created for the population as a whole, as well as for tourists.

Facilities such as the cable car in the Favelas do Alemão complex, the Manguinhos promenade, the Santa Marta funicular and the lift in Cantagalo are encouraging new uses and ways of access to the *favelas*, so that once inconceivable kinds of activity can develop there.

Besides the *favela* tourism offered by travel agencies in the *favelas*, there are new eating places that are gradually being absorbed and integrated into the city's range of amenities, along with cyclo-cross tournaments, theatre and dance performances and other activities. New places to eat are mentioned daily in formal and informal advertising across the city. On the fringes of the Babilônia *favela*, in the Leme neighbourhood of Rio's Copacabana district, there are restaurants serving special dishes for tourists and students who want to get to know '*favela* life' at first hand. And, as of New Year's Eve 2010, Cantagalo now offers an all-in package including the New Year fireworks and a special New Year's Eve dinner.

However, there is a risk that such changes may encourage the cosmopolitanization of urban policy and lead to the disappearance of productive activities – a trend that will restrict the use of cities to housing, culture, tourism and services, and reduce the older processing and production sectors to mere memories or push them out to peripheral areas (whether in 'developed' countries or ones that are themselves peripheral). Today's megacities are tending to become service cities.

In places where there used to be fishing boats, there are now plans for aquariums and fishing-themed walks and hotels. Where there used to be industry, there are now industry-themed bars, discotheques, bookshops and creative businesses. Where there used to be agriculture, there are now educational farms and agriculture-themed health-food restaurants.

Urban production areas are thus often being turned into service, culture and leisure areas, based on urban concepts in which now-abandoned activities are presented as themes, often without proper regard for the actual activities or the skills associated with them. Let me make clear that I am not calling here for the revival of some nostalgic or bucolic notion of urban production. Urban production, whether in agriculture, fishing or industry, must adapt to technical progress and remain compatible with other urban functions. Whereas during the Industrial Revolution such activities were mainly seen as sources of pollution, technological progress is now enabling us to rediscover compatibilities and links between functions that have been driven out of cities and ones that have not – livestock and housing, vegetable gardens and restaurants, industry and leisure, and so on.

In Rocinha, besides the vast number of local restaurants frequented by people from both inside and outside the *favela*, there is a staircase in a private house that leads up to the roof of a house owned by someone else and known as A Lage, where events, parties and celebrations are held and specially prepared meals and drinks are available – always including *feijoada completa*, Brazil's famous bean stew.

One explanation for the name Rocinha goes back to the 1920s, when the neighbouring Gávea district had a fruit and vegetable market that was renowned for the quality of its produce. When the vendors were asked by customers where they got their fine vegetables from, they would reply 'from my *rocinha* (little garden)'. Today Rocinha is home to more than 100,000 people who live in some 20,000 dwellings scattered over 20 subdistricts. *Feijoada*, a blend of ingredients and flavours originally derived from the food eaten in the slave quarters on the former colonial estates, has since developed to the point where it is now served everywhere, from five-star hotels to simple corner *botecos*. It has become an integral part of Rio's culinary 'spirit'.

The dish varies throughout Brazil, depending on local ingredients and the type of beans available in each region of the country. An invitation to eat *feijoada* is a mark of friendship, and refusal to accept would be considered rude, for eating *feijoada* is a participatory, socially inclusive event.

The way in which *feijoada* is presented, whether in a restaurant or in the homes of friends or acquaintances, always involves the eyes and sense of smell, and is a ceremony (or ritual) that makes guests feel they are taking part in what is virtually a family occasion. Its presentation at the table involves a series of components and ingredients of various kinds and sizes. The rice is served in small dishes that are the size of ordinary plates and are distributed over the table, whereas the beans are served in numerous clay pots that keep them at the right temperature. The cabbage and *farofa* (toasted manioc flour, of which there are many different versions) are also served in their own special vessels. The table is filled with an abundance of food, conveying the joy of being alive and being part of a feast.

The natural, varied ingredients of *feijoada* whet the appetite, whether one belongs to the more privileged or less privileged sectors of society. The classic *caipirinha* cocktail on arrival and the generous supply of beer during the meal encourage conversation. The whole thing is a mini-odyssey of food, experienced through the eyes. The visual presentation has no centre – instead, the various ingredients are arranged as a set of fragments, none of which is superior to the others by virtue of its position on the table or its relative importance.

In urban design, just as with *feijoada*, there are no fixed recipes – the answers vary from place to place. It has to be grasped in all its various layers, centres and ways of presentation. So the project must start by reading local conditions, listening to people's requirements, interacting with other fields of knowledge and providing the backbone of the changes that are required. Today's ideal urban design would thus offer interconnected places like so many contemporary New Agoras, in which work, housing and recreation are interwoven in an inside-outside continuum, as in Fellini's *Roma*, turning the street into a living room that provides space for user-friendliness and coexistence.

What we need to reconsider today is the relationship between **the city** (*a spatial configuration defined by the establishment of permanent buildings and inhabited by a numerous, dense, heterogeneous population largely made up of strangers*), **urbanity** (*a way of life marked by mobility, agitation as a source of social structuring and the proliferation of relational networks – a society that usually moves and is occasionally mobilized*) and **public space** (*surfaces in which shifts occur and lead to an infinite number of intersections and junctions – a setting for human agitation in which political and cultural dimensions are at the centre of all issues* (Manuel Delgado).

Today's cities suffer from a lack of congregational spaces where their inhabitants can meet and share and swap experiences, interests, products and knowledge, in a physical setting that encourages social life. What we lack today are collective spaces that are suitable for carrying on all kinds of socially inclusive activities and are interconnected by non-polluting, efficient, high-quality public transport.

The 21st-century city has to be friendly, democratic, inclusive, green and fertile.

Today we must review the relationship between what Lucio Costa called the 'green mass' and the 'built mass' and redirect it towards a new 'urban nature' and a new 'social contract' in which the reorientation of behaviour can generate more favourable settings for the lives of every creature on our planet and ensure less suffering for both humans and animals.

An architect's 'social function' – including my own – is to be a 'provider of services' that first of all considers the interests (the logic) of the whole city and then the interests of the public or private client, individually or collectively, without giving priority to any of these elements, sometimes at the risk of losing the assignment. This is because there is a close relationship between ethics doing what needs to be done), aesthetics (the challenge of the new) and politics (the ever-difficult relationships between power structures), and because architects and urban planners always have to deal with compromise, conflict, interference and change.

Whether in the *favelas* or the official city, at the Morro do Adeus cable car station in the Favelas do Alemão complex or in artist Caio Blat's home, my projects always include spaces for the ceremony of eating, so as to create 'spatial settings' in which people at the table can enjoy both food and conversation in a setting that is geared to the landscape – 'consumption of place' being more important than 'place of consumption'. 'Making the landscape available' in this way is one of the services that architects must surely offer. In this sense, the didactic dimension of the act of eating in company with others while incorporating the landscape is one of the features that distinguishes Rio de Janeiro from other cities, whether one is rich or poor, living in the favelas or the official city, the *morro* (slums) or the *asfalto* (white-collar districts). Enhancing the presence of nature in the city through the act of eating, if possible in well-shaded and naturally ventilated indoor or outdoor settings, is one way of contributing to Paquot's existential ecology.

Through our projects, we architects and urban planners can encourage a way of living that is better geared to coexistence between differences and enjoyment of the environment, in a well-balanced blend of nature and artifice, an interweaving of architecture and setting in which food can be enjoyed with friends, outdoors as well as indoors.

It is in the architect-client relationship that the potential of the project must be constructed through dialogue; and that is why the architect's work includes a 'didactic' dimension regarding a project's ability to 'show', i.e. to make clear to the other person what he was 'entitled to want' but was unaware of 'before the dialogue'. Every project thus acquires a special meaning that makes it – just like food – an integral part of the field of culture.

To end with Arnaldo Antunes's song *Comida* (Food)

'We don't just want food
We want food,
entertainment and art
We don't just want food
We want a way out
To anywhere'

Case Study Food Miles per Commodity

Food miles are the number of miles food travels to the consumer. Global data on food miles are still scarce.
Here, we present figures from California, showing related greenhouse gases emissions.

Source: NRDC, *NRDC food miles fact sheets: methodology and sources*. Natural resources defence council, (California: 2007). Online.
Available http://www.nrdc.org/health/effects/camiles/methodology.pdf (accessed 15 February 2012).

 250 Miles

Table Grapes Chile by Ship   Tons Imported 129,721 | Greenhouse Gases 7343 tons/yr | Smog Forming Pollutants 298 tons/yr

●●●●●●●●●●●●●●●●●●●●●●●●(

Food Miles 5909

Navel Oranges Australia by Ship   Tons Imported 33,095 | Greenhouse Gases 2628 tons/yr | Smog Forming Pollutants 76 tons/yr

●●●●●●●●●●●●●●●●●●●●●●●●●●●●●●●●●●●●(

Food Miles 8655

Wine France by Ship   Tons Imported 47,464 | Greenhouse Gases 5084 tons/yr | Smog Forming Pollutants 109 tons/yr

●●●(

Food Miles 10,361

Garlic China by Ship   Tons Imported 24,610 | Greenhouse Gases 2185 tons/yr | Smog Forming Pollutants 57 tons/yr

●●●●●●●●●●●●●●●●●●●●●●●●●●●●●(

Food Miles 7333

Rice Thailand by Ship   Tons Imported 207,374 | Greenhouse Gases 15,394 tons/yr | Smog Forming Pollutants 477 tons/yr

●●●●●●●●●●●●●●●●●●●●●●●●●●●●●●●●●

Food Miles 8229

Fresh Tomatoes Mexico by Truck   Tons Imported 90,096 | Greenhouse Gases 7649 tons/yr | Smog Forming Pollutants 8 tons/yr

●●●●(

Food Miles 1193

Fresh Tomatoes Netherlands by Airplane   Tons Imported 830 | Greenhouse Gases 6482 tons/yr | Smog Forming Pollutants 0,2 tons/yr

●●●●●●●●●●●●●●●●●●●●●●

Food Miles 5727

Biofuels Compete with Food

The outcome of the modelled decrease in calorie availability (%) by 2020 in different regions of the world under two biofuel expansion scenarios. In scenario one the assumption is that the current biofuel plans of involved countries will be realized. In scenario two the expansion of the production of scenario one is doubled.

Source: J. Von Braun (2007), *When food makes fuel: the promises and challenges of biofuels*, Keynote address at the Crawford Fund Annual Conference, Australia. IFPRI, Washington DC.

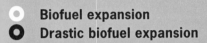

Biofuel expansion
Drastic biofuel expansion

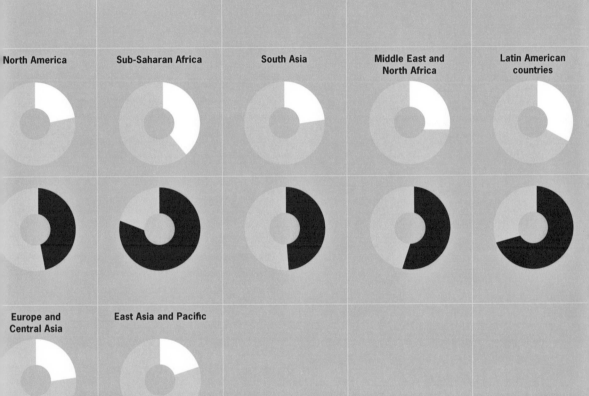

| North America | Sub-Saharan Africa | South Asia | Middle East and North Africa | Latin American countries |

| Europe and Central Asia | East Asia and Pacific |

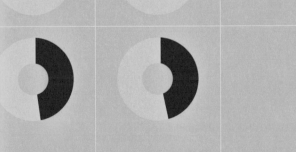

135

Transportation and Distribution

page 137

Pig transport in the province of Brabant, the Netherlands, one of the largest exporters of live pigs, piglets, and pork in the world. In 2010, more than 7000 Dutch pig farmers kept 12.2 million pigs. Every day 30,000 pigs are put on transport to other countries, mainly in Europe but with growing markets in Russia and South Korea as well.

Photo: Dolph Cantrijn, 2004. Source: Hollandse Hoogte

page 138-139

Caravan in Ethiopia with camels carrying salt.

Photo: Pascal Boegli, 2008. Source: pbOOg.cOm

page 140

Transport of live chicken in Burkina Faso.

Photo: Ferdinand Reus. Source: Wikimedia Commons

page 141

Traders work the crude oil options pit at the New York Mercantile Exchange, Friday August 5, 2011. Global oil prices are rising as investors worry about another global recession.

Photo: Mary Altaffer. Source: Reporters / AP

page 142-143

In the political film essay *The Forgotten Space* the American artist Allan Sekula and American film director Noël Burch follow container cargo aboard ships, trains and trucks around the globe and talk to people who are marginalized by the global transport system.

Still: Allan Sekula & Noël Burch. Source: DocEye

page 144-145

In the high-tech traffic control centre of the Rotterdam harbour, traffic controllers monitor all ship movements on the Nieuwe Maas river. About 430 million tons of goods pass the Rotterdam port each year; the port is also the gateway to the European market of more than 350 million consumers.

Photo: Rob Huibers, 2010. Source: Hollandse Hoogte

page 146

Warehouse with bags of rice from India in the seaport of Matadi, Democratic Republic of Congo.

Photo: Carl de Keyzer, in the series *Congo*, 2007. Source: Magnum Photos

[page 147

British retailer Sainsbury's, with 557 supermarkets and 377 convenience stores, is supplied by 23 regional distribution centres. This RDG is located at Waltham Point in Essex and measures 700,000 sq ft, the equivalent of 267 tennis courts. Four-and-a-half miles of conveyor belts, with 200 different belts in use, handle 3 million cases each week. The vulnerability of these centres for outside threats such as agroterrorism, E.coli outbreaks or delivery problems due to volcanic outbursts or other natural disasters has been increasingly commented upon.

Photo: Nick Saltmarsh, 2004. Source: Flickr.com

page 148-149

The distribution centre of the largest American grocery retailer Wal-Mart Stores Inc. in Spring Valley, Illinois, USA opened its doors in March 2001 and is one of the company's 130 centres. Functioning until 2011 as a regional centre for local distribution, the centre could process and move 20,000 cases of goods per hour. Wal-Mart has 8,500 stores in 15 countries, with 55 different names. Critics worry about the effect of Wal-marts stores on local communities.

Photo: Daniel Acker, 2011. Source: Bloomberg via Getty Images

page 150

American artist Adam Purple was ahead of his time when he created his earthwork *Garden of Eden* in Manhattan's Lower East Side from 1975 to 1986. Over a period of five years Purple transformed five lots of brick rubble to topsoil with horse manure from Central Park. The circular garden produced edible corn, cucumbers, tomatoes, raspberries and strawberries. In January 1986 the city bulldozed the community garden and put up low-rise apartment buildings.

Photo and source: Harvey Wang

page 151
The global design agency Philips Design designed a self-contained 'home farm' that could grow part of a family's food needs inside the house. The system, with a closed loop using natural principles like the channelling of natural light, using shrimp to purify the water and fish to fertilize the plants, should source part of our food in 15-20 years' time.
Photo and source: Philips Design – Biosphere Home Farming, part of Philips Design Food probe

page 152
The European Union allocated € 2.5 million to FAO for agri-cultural rehabilitation in Togo, after floods ravaged crops and killed livestock in 2007, raising food prices and aggravating the livelihoods of the rural population. Particularly nursing and pregnant women were affected: they received seeds and training for market gardening.
Photo: Giulio Napolitano. Source: Food and Agriculture Organization in the series 'Togo: return on investment'

How to Think and Farm Out of the Box

An interview with Annechien ten Have-Mellema by Brigitte van der Sande

The Farmer
Annechien ten Have-Mellema

The Dutch farmer Annechien ten Have-Mellema is not your
typical agriculturalist: the scale of her farm of 300 hectares
is in itself enormous compared to the average 24,2 hectares
in the Netherlands. More intriguing however is her open-
minded approach to the challenges of farming in this day and
age. To her a future as a vegetarian meat producer is not at
all inconceivable.

When Annechien Mellema told her mother that she wanted to become a farmer just like her parents, her mother was not immediately enthusiastic. As an intelligent woman with a college education who had married a farmer herself, she knew what awaited her daughter: hard work and an insecure income. Annechien got her Diploma in Education and worked for a few years as a teacher, but fate came to the rescue when she fell in love with a farmer and her dream came true.

Annechien's parents were visionary people. Her father had inherited a farm of 67 hectares in Beerta with both arable land and dairy farming, as was customary on the fertile clay in the northeast of the Netherlands, near the German border. He and his ten farmhands milked the cows, put them out to pasture, made hay and harvested crops, not unlike his predecessors in biblical times. In the 1950s and 1960s, European Commissioner of Agriculture Sicco Mansholt however stimulated farmers to specialize and expand, and he created land consolidation laws to join scattered plots of land that traditionally belonged to many different farmers. Large-scale intensive farming became the new policy, and when the European Economic Community, the EU's predecessor, guaranteed the price of agrarian produce, livestock and arable farming in the Netherlands in particular grew explosively. Annechien's parents decided to specialize in arable farming and parted with their cows. Due to the ever-increasing automation and scaling-up farmers could work so efficiently that they could manage the farm without extra labourers. Knowing they would have to sack their last farm-hand, Annechien's parents chose to start farming pigs on a large scale, which was rather exceptional in their region, known as the Grain Republic. In hindsight it was a wise decision: many of the farmers who stuck with wheat either gave up farming or emigrated.

Annechien and her husband Menno ten Have took over the small mixed farm of her parents-in-law in the east of the country, but when her own parents decided to stop in 1993, Annechien and her husband moved back to the open polder landscape of her youth. On the day they arrived her uncle died and the Ten Haves bought his land, creating a farm of 200 hectares, later expanded to 300 hectares through land lease. Even for this region this can be considered an extensive farm, but on a national scale it is enormous: the average was 24,2 hectares in 2010.

The Ten Have farm is quite exceptional in the Netherlands, as where most farmers specialize in one culture, their farm has three branches that 'feed' each other: arable farming, pigs, and biogas. The maize and wheat on the fields is fed to the pigs, the pig manure goes into the biogas installation, together with leftover agricultural products such as onions and potatoes from neighbouring farms. The residual product of this mash, the digestate, is used as a fertilizer on the land. The biogas installation currently has a capacity of 0,6 megawatt, delivering electricity to 1100 households and heating the piggeries that hold 8000 pigs yearly. The Ten Haves have plans to extend the capacity to 1,1 megawatt and, together with a food technologist and a dried vegetable company, are researching the potential of a new technique to use the biogas to dry fruit, vegetables, and meat.

No part of the pig, whose lifespan from birth to slaughterhouse is six months, is wasted: each and every pig contributes to 120 food and non-food products. Only 54 of the more than 100 kilos stay on the local market in the 'Pure and Honest' house brand of one of the two large national retailers, the rest of the pig's parts are sent all over the world to be processed. Feet, tails and ears go to China to be eaten, while heart valves find their way into the hearts of people all over Europe. Glue, chinaware, insulin, sweets, cosmetics, soap, tooth paste, paint, candles, hair brushes and paint brushes all contain parts of the bones, organs, hide, hair, blood or lard of pigs. The Ten Haves' target to maximize the economic value of each pig means that it is impossible, now or in the future, to sell 100% of the pig in the home market, even if the Dutch change their menu. The local and global markets are more and more interconnected and this trend will continue, in their opinion.

With the increasing domination of neo-liberal politicians who believe in the self-regulation of the market and the growing influence of animal protection groups and environmental organizations on public awareness, the profession of farming has become a challenging one. Farmers think in the long term, and they invest for periods of 20 to 25 years. Politicians, on the contrary, usually don't think further than the next elections, which is four years at best. A complicating factor is the interdependency of national agricultural and economic policies with the political power of the European Union. As chair of the Section Pig Farming of LTO, (the main Dutch Farmers Organization) and vice-chair of the Product Boards for Livestock and Meat, Annechien meets with stakeholders of the agricultural sector four times a week to discuss the future of local food production and consumption in an increasingly global economy. If it is true that eating is voting with your fork, as the much quoted New York Times contributor Michael Pollan wrote in his book *The Omnivore's Dilemma. A Natural History of Four Meals* (2006), then the mechanisms of the whole food chain should become transparent, claims Annechien. It is not the farmer, as the first link in the chain, who decides what to produce, nor does the consumer, as the last link, determine what is sold in the supermarkets. In between there are many links that are today more decisive, such as the retailers and their strategic buying alliances like AMS, who are the gatekeepers of the European food system and in 2010 had a combined retail sales value of 127 billion euro.

The one and only woman in a high executive position in the agricultural world, Annechien joins hands with former opponents such as animal protection groups and environmental NGO's to improve the living conditions of the animals, find solutions for pollution and health issues, and she represents her members in negotiations and talks with retailers, politicians, ministries and other players in the field. Inch by inch, Annechien and her colleagues are trying to transform the old agricultural policies into a sustainable agriculture, where economic values match ecological and social values. A good example of such a newly formed coalition is the trial project *ComfortClass* for pigs, a collaboration between the Dutch Federation of Agriculture and Horticulture, the Society for Animal Protection, Wageningen UR Livestock Research, the cooperative feed manufacturer ForFarmers and Privon, the Foundation for Intensive Livestock Farming. *ComfortClass* seeks to find a balance between a fair price for the farmers and the well-being of the pig. Five pig farmers in different parts of the country, including Annechien and her husband, started the *ComfortClass* experiment in 2005 to test the implications of a pig-friendly piggery, based upon the ten basic needs of a pig: saturation, tranquillity, exploration, social contact, shitting and urinating, grating, scratching and grubbing, exercise, health, thermocomfort and safety. The Ten Haves renovated four departments of the old piggery, with more square meters for each pig and more pigs in a group, mash feeding in long troughs, toys to play with, a sprinkler installation for hot days and skylights in the roof to bring light in the stalls. The initial investment is much higher than for a standard piggery, but the Ten Haves are even going to expand the experiment with new investments in piggeries that also have an open connection with outside spaces, and straw on the floor, offering the pigs more freedom of choice and a more natural environment. Tentatively they will start feeding the pigs lupin, the beautiful blue ornamental flower that can be grown in moderate and cool climates and that is increasingly recognized as an alternative to the usual protein pig feed of soy, which has to be imported from South America. Again the Ten Haves will create a cycle with the pig manure as fertilizer for the fields of locally grown lupin, and the lupin as feed for the pigs. Lupin can be grown without using herbicides for crop protection, which is another advantage, not to mention the more elegant taste of the meat of the lupin pig. The most decisive factor for success though is if the retailers will start selling this meat, and if consumers will be prepared to pay a higher price.

The most fundamental issue in the transition to a sustainable and animal-friendly agrarian industry, according to Annechien, is restoring the broken relationship between farmer and consumer in the Western world. Consumers in the city hardly have a clue what a farmer does. The only contact is through the media, which usually means bad news: images of mega stalls with sows that can't move, people with masks against bird flu, and death statistics when one bacteria or virus after the other spreads over the world like the bubonic plague in earlier times. Add to these palpable images less visible threats like climate change, water pollution etc., and you'll understand that in the mind of the average consumer farming has become a peril, an uncontrollable activity that should be put as far away as possible. With the exception of course of the small farms where pigs roll in the mud, calves frolic in the meadow and the farmer's children ride happily into the sunset on their ponies. This romantic view of farming is paradoxical: most people are not prepared to pay realistic prices for food, so food comes from afar where it is cheapest, or is produced in mega quantities with all the known consequences. At the same time, people abhor mega stalls and monoculture farming and they demand absolute control over the side effects of farming, which are actually easier to manage in intensive livestock farming than in organic farming.

The farmer on the other hand does not know what the consumer wants, because he has handed over his power to co-ops, whose original task of representing small farmers evolved into a power structure in itself, sales and marketing included, minimizing the position of the individual farmer in the process. Co-ops should maintain close ties with their founder-members, even when they become large multinationals. Farmers should get out of the stalls and sties and restore the bonds they traditionally had with their markets. That means meeting up with slaughterers and butchers, shopkeepers and retailers, animal protection groups and environmental NGO's, and researching local and global markets and developments, in short, creating new and strong ties between *boer and burgher*, i.e. farmer and citizen. With experiments like the lupin pig, farmers such as the Ten Haves zero in on an emerging market for food that can be situated between the standard and organic products, and they expect that other retailers will jump on the bandwagon.

Since her youth, Annechien has seen the farming community in her region change drastically. The old arable farms have disappeared and the boarded-up and ramshackle buildings remain as silent witnesses. Many young farmers emigrated to Canada in the eighties and nineties, where they expected less regulation, less laws and less red tape than in the Netherlands. Due to zoning changes and the growing urbanization of other parts of the country, many intensive dairy farmers have moved to her region since the end of the nineties, together with the odd artist or hippie who appreciates the open and empty landscape of Groningen province. Agriculture has been recognized as one of the main engines of economical activity in these rural areas, creating work and opportunities for young people who otherwise would leave in search of jobs. Not many Dutch realize that the Netherlands are the second largest exporter of agricultural products in the world, after the United States, with a revenue of 65 billion euro in 2010.

The contribution Annechien wrote in 2010 for the Dutch language website foodlog.nl on the research of large-scale use of algae for protein, is typical for her way of thinking. Presented as a feasible and tasty alternative to the hamburger, the algae burger could threaten her family's livelihood and many farmers would oppose to such a development, or ignore it, as farmers have done in the past with margarine. Not Annechien. Algae eat phosphate and nitrate. With the phosphate and nitrate in pig shit Annechien could produce about twice as much meat, pig and vegetarian, as she does now. She ends her blog with a key question: if she accepts the alternatives for meat, will vegetarians accept her as a vegetarian meat producer?

Annechien and Menno are clearly not your average farming couple that meekly follows the national and European agricultural policies, but are in the vanguard of the experimental agriculture, seeking a balance between an economically healthy business and a sustainable future for their farm. Their son Detmer is already responsible for the biogas development of their farm and will hopefully take the farm over, in due time. Their daughter Lizeth has started a medical training but lends a hand when necessary. Choice or fate, Annechien foresees a prolific future for sustainable agriculture.

Solving the Problems of Food Production in 2050 through Synthetic Genomics Technology

The Technologists

James H. Flatt, George E. Stagnitti, Ari Patrinosi[1] and J. Craig Venter[2]

With a prognosis of a world population of 9 billion in 2050 the American pioneers of genomic research Dr. J. Craig Venter and his colleagues reason that synthetic genomic technologies will be vital to a sustainable global food system. Synthetic chromosomes will greatly reduce the time to develop food-producing microbes, plants and animals.[3]

Consider a typical dinner which might be served in the year 2050, and how it might differ from what is served today. The meal starts with a locally-sourced salad, dressed with a healthy, high monounsaturated oil derived from bioengineered photosynthetic microalgae. The main course features grilled salmon, sourced from aquaculture farms using microalgae in place of fish meal, which is scarce due to prolonged decline in fisheries. Alternatively, one could choose a vegetarian chicken analogue main dish, produced from texturized, bioengineered single cell protein sources, and virtually indistinguishable in taste and texture from real chicken. The roasted Russet potato starch is enriched with beneficial carotenoids and antioxidant nutrients found in the sweet potato, achieved through molecular breeding. Not only will it be possible to develop all of these products by 2050 through application of synthetic genomic technologies, it will also a be necessity if the world is to sustain a population of 9 billion in the year 2050 in good health.

Genomics is the study of the structure and function of genetic elements, which are the software of living organisms. Synthetic genomics combines methods for the chemical synthesis of DNA with computational techniques to design DNA. Synthetic genomic methods allow scientists to construct genetic material that would be impossible or impractical to produce using more conventional biotechnological approaches. Foods that are healthier, and produced on marginal land with fewer chemical inputs with yields that that will support a growing population, will be enabled by synthetic genomic technologies.

A Critical Need

The challenge of feeding a growing population with healthier alternatives in an environmentally sustainable manner is significant. Consider the facts. The Food and Agriculture Organization estimates that the worldwide food supply will need to increase by 70% by 2050.[4] However, it is not only caloric need that must be met, but also the need for healthier foods that will reduce the risk of chronic diseases such as cardiovascular disease and diabetes, which will impair quality of life and create an unbearable economic burden on the worldwide health care system.[5]

These goals must be achieved in the face of several long-term constraints that add to the challenge. First, the availability of cultivatable land is limited and will be further restricted by competing demand from a growing population and climate change, which may result in an actual reduction in cultivated land area by 2050.[6] Second, the growing worldwide demand for animal protein, a trend that is correlated with economic development, will intensify the need for primary food sources. The production of 1 kilogram of animal protein requires 10 kilograms of vegetable or microbial protein and 15,000 litres of water.[7] A similar situation exists with respect to fish supply, where a thirty-year lack of growth in wild fish harvest has driven a growing demand for farmed fish.[8] Third, the availability of essential nutrients, such as nitrogen, phosphorus and non-brackish water, will be limited and increasingly costly.[9]

This constraint will severely limit the world's ability to achieve higher crop yields through the chemically-intensive agronomic practices that have been utilized in developed countries to drive improvement. It is estimated that the combined effects of climate change, land degradation, cropland losses, water scarcity and species infestations may cause projected yields to be 5–25% short of demand by 2050.[10]

Synthetic Genomic Technology Solutions

Meeting the challenge of providing sufficient food will require implementation of all available methods, including synthetic genomics, to enhance productivity of existing food sources, and the development of entirely new food sources. Let's consider how synthetic genomic technologies will be applied to develop improved or novel plant, animal, and microbial food sources.

Terrestrial Crops

The introduction of genetically engineered crops in the 1990s highlighted the yield improvement promise afforded by this technology but also environmental and public acceptance concerns that will have to be addressed before broader-scale adoption of this technology. Initial plant genetic engineering efforts involved introduction of single genes to inhibit insect damage (e.g. Bt toxin) or facilitate use of broad-spectrum herbicides (e.g. glyphosate resistance) for a limited number of high acreage crops, such as corn, soybean and rapeseed canola. Synthetic genomics technologies will be required to consolidate the larger number of simultaneous genetic changes, or 'stacked traits', required for further yield improvement.

2050 Prediction: Major food-producing crops will be 'semi-synthetic', containing at least one synthetic chromosome, which encodes genes driving multiple beneficial traits, including enhanced photosynthetic efficiency, drought resistance, salt tolerance and production of beneficial micronutrients. These synthetic chromosomes will be introduced into a variety of genetic backgrounds that are better suited for growth in broader geographical regions. Conventional breeding techniques will be a thing of the past, replaced by molecular breeding techniques in which plant variants are crossed based upon a priori knowledge of differences in their respective genomic sequences. Molecular breeding will be utilized in a variety of cereal grain and vegetable crops, including sorghum, pearl millet, quinoa, potatoes, tomatoes and beans.

Microbial Food Sources

A number of commonly used food ingredients are produced using natural, classically-improved and genetically modified microorganisms. Ingredients produced by microbial fermentation include amino acids, acidulants (e.g. citric acid), texturizing ingredients (e.g. xanthan gum), enzymes and colourants. A fungal microorganism, Fusarium venenatum, is the source of a vegetarian, but expensive, protein source, Quorn™, which is increasingly available in packaged food products .[11]

2050 Prediction: Cultivated, highly-productive photosynthetic microalgae will become a major new food and feed ingredient source. These simple plants will be 'semi-synthetic' or 'wholly synthetic', designed to produce macronutrients and micronutrients with significantly higher productivity and areal yield than natural counterparts. A single cell 'algalbean' will provide a renewable and sustainable supply of oil, flour and protein for use as food and feed ingredients. Why microalgae? Microalgae are simple, single-cell plants which can achieve significantly higher areal productivities on marginal land with non-potable water and limited nutrient inputs. Current oil and protein yields of natural microalgae already are several-fold higher than achieved in terrestrial crops, and can theoretically go much higher with appropriate engineering. Economic modelling indicates that achievement of the yields can result in production costs comparable to projected costs of producing traditional crops. Furthermore, microalgae are inherently excellent sources of beneficial nutrients including long-chain polyunsaturated omega-3 fatty acids, carotenoids, antioxidants and certain vitamins.[12]

Development of algae crops will however require significant engineering to further increase yield necessary for cost reduction, tailoring nutritional, taste and texture profiles for consumption by animals and humans, and provide measures for appropriate biocontainment.

Meat-Producing Animals

Land animals and fish used as food sources are exclusively the product of natural or conventional breeding. Recent scientific advances leading to the introduction of genes in multiple animal species and cloning of whole organisms has generated speculation as to the potential of using transgenic animals as food sources. Two developments of note include reports of a transgenic pig modified to have a healthier, omega-3 fatty acid rich profile[13] and a transgenic Chinook salmon modified to grow twice as fast as its natural counterpart.[14]

2050 Prediction: Analogous to the situation described for terrestrial crops, bioengineered animals exhibiting faster growth rates, improved yield on costly feed ingredients and providing healthier sources of meat protein will be readily available in 2050. Reducing the amount of saturated fat with commensurate increase in the amount of monounsaturated and polyunsaturated fat, and partially replacing cholesterol with plant sterols are likely targets of genetic engineering efforts.

Nutrigenomics- Emerging Science in 2050

Ground-breaking insight generated from the Human Genome Project and follow-on research will have broad application across the food and nutrition industries. The science of nutrigenomics has evolved to describe how foods affect our genes and how individual differences in gene sequences result in differential responses to nutrients and components of the diet. Nutrients also impact gene expression and

163

metabolism of the human microbiome community, thereby influencing the course of nutrition related disorders such as diabetes, obesity, cardiovascular disease, hypertension, osteoarthritis and many inflammation driven disorders.

The requirement for and the ability to deliver more precisely directed food and nutritional product solutions have improved with our growing understanding of differences in the genetic makeup of individuals. Customized nutritional or medical food products to address specific dietary needs for disease prevention will become increasingly available later in this decade.

As scientific research continues to clarify and substantiate the linkage between genetic makeup, nutrients and health benefit, it is imperative not to lose sight of several important industry and consumer needs that are central to determining the ultimate success and acceptance of the technology. These needs include maintaining or improving product efficacy, and sensory qualities. Products must be safe, effective, stable and deliver a high level of quality throughout their expected shelf life. As new technologies develop, a high degree of regulatory compliance continues to be essential.

Required Technology Advances

Further significant advances in synthetic genomic technologies will be required to realize these predictions. First, the cost of synthesizing and assembling DNA must drop by two orders of magnitude to facilitate large-scale engineering of microbial, plant and animal food sources. DNA synthesis and assembly costs are projected to decrease significantly during this decade. Low cost must be achieved with high accuracy, in systems where even one error in the genome may be lethal.[15] Second, more robust methods of introducing and activating synthetic chromosomes in higher organisms must be developed. Third, our knowledge of how the genetic sequence impacts organism function must increase exponentially in order to inform rational engineering or breeding of food-producing organisms and develop nutritional products tailored to genetically-clustered groups of consumers. Having the tools to build an organism is insufficient; we must also know how to build one that is better.

Bioethics – Responsible Use of Synthetic Genomics Technologies

The use of synthetic biology to produce foods needs to be governed by strong bioethics standards. The experiences of recombinant DNA technologies and particularly the early introduction of GMO's in agriculture are very instructive in this respect. The 'lesson learned' from those experiences mandates the adoption of practices that enable the public acceptance of synthetic genomics in the production of foods. For example, it is imperative to anticipate the concerns from governments, NGO's and the public and to demonstrate complete and thorough transparency of the processes involved in the production of such foods. We must communicate early and often the results of specific studies that are undertaken to confirm the safety of the generated products. Advances in synthetic genomics prompted the Obama Administration to seek guidance on the ethics of synthetic genomics and emerging technologies.[16] The Bioethics Commission identified five ethical principles they considered relevant to social acceptance of such technologies: public beneficence, responsible stewardship, intellectual freedom and responsibility, democratic deliberation; and justice and fairness.

The Bioethics Commission provided a total of eighteen detailed recommendations for future applications of synthetic genomics, many of which would be applicable for the application of synthetic genomics in the production of food. The recommendations ranged from the definitions of the proper institutions and processes to oversee synthetic genomics applications to specific studies of associated risk assessments of synthetic genomics practices.

Summary
Synthetic genomics technologies will enable accelerated development of species utilized for food, which show enhanced productivity in a land, water and carbon resource constrained world. By 2050, technology advances will enable the engineering of synthetic chromosomes carrying the beneficial traits of interest in a matter of days, greatly reducing the time to develop preferred food-producing microbes, plants and animals.

Global Meat Demand Towards 2020

Global meat demand (in million metric tons) in developed and developing countries in 1974 and 1997, and the expected global meat demand in 2020. The 55% increase in global meat demand will be accounted for mostly by China (40%). Note that these figures are absolute. The demand per capita in 2020 remains higher for developed countries than for developing countries.

Source: M.W. Rosegrant, M.S. Paisner, S. Meijer and J. Witcover, *2020 global food outlook. Trends, alternatives, and choices* (Washington DC: International Food Policy Research Institute, 2001)

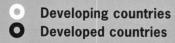 Developing countries
Developed countries

World 1974
109 million metric tons

World 1997
208 million metric tons

World 2020
327 million metric tons

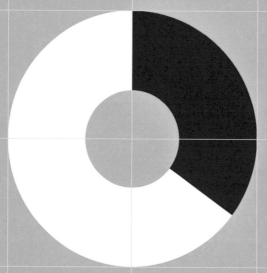

Epidemic Hazards

The number of epidemic events in the world reported between 1980 and 2008.

Source: EM-DAT, *The international disaster database.* Online. Available http://www.emdat.be/ (accessed 15 February 2012).

1984   1985   1986   1987   1988

1989   1990   1991   1992   1993

1994   1995   1996   1997   1998

1999   2000   2001   2002   2003

2004   2005   2006   2007   2008

Consumption

177

179

page 182 top

Activists of Food Grain Godown Workers Union eat leaves as they protest in favour of their demands, on October 25, 2010 in Hyderabad.

Photo: Asianet-Pakistan, 2010. Source: Shutterstock.

page 182, bottom

Exactly 27 years after the first bread riots in 1984 in Tunisia, new anti-government protests forced Tunisian President Zine El Abidine Ben Ali to flee to Saudi Arabia. A wave of protests and demonstrations spread across North Africa and the Middle East, toppling governments and dictators in what was coined as the Arab Spring or Arab Awakening. The two slogans of the Arab Spring 'bread, freedom and dignity' and 'the people demand the fall/change of the order' haven't lost their appeal yet.

Photo: Hassene Dridi, 2011. Source: Reporters/AP

page 183 top

When the North American Free Trade Agreement (NAFTA) removed import tariffs on farm goods from the US and Canada in January 2008, demonstrators in Mexico went to the streets with an enormous corn cob. Many experts believe that governments should invest in small farmers, instead of letting them drown in the waves of global agribusiness.

Photo: Eduardo Verdugo. Source: Reporters/AP

page 183 bottom

Protesters in South Korea clash with riot police near the presidential house in Seoul in June 2008, after the government's decision to resume imports of American beef. Weeks of anti-government protests were sparked by people's concerns over food safety, in particular 'mad cow' disease.

Photo: Ahn Young-Joon, 2008. Source: Reporters/AP

page 184

Stranded migrant workers from Egypt, Bangladesh, Vietnam, Ghana, the Philippines and other countries who have fled the violence in Libya wait for food distribution in a refugee camp near the Tunisian/Egyptian border.

Photo: Alvarra Ybarra Zavala, 2011. Source: Getty Images

Seed to Table:
Navdanya's Innovation in Enhancing Food Security in the City and the Villages

The Activist

Dr. Vandana Shiva with Maya Goburdhun

Founder Vandana Shiva and director Maya Goburdhun of the network of seed keepers and organic producers Navdanya, active across 16 states in India, illuminate their continuous efforts to create an agriculture that is based upon principles of equity, i.e. Food for All. Gandhi's motto 'Be the change we seek to see' lies at the base of Navdanya's philosophy that citizens have the responsibility to act when political will is non-existent.

I started the women-led nature-centred Navdanya Movement 25 years ago in response to the emerging threats to biodiversity and food security from genetic engineering and patents on seeds and life. Navdanya means 'nine seeds'. It also means 'new gift'. Nine seeds stand for diversity and the new gift we bring are seeds of life, seeds of freedom, and seeds of hope.

One of the dominant myths of our times is that we need industrial agriculture to produce more food. However, industrial agriculture does not produce more food, it produces more commodities, and commodities do not feed people. The world is growing huge quantities of genetically modified corn and soya. The biotechnology industry would have us believe that this has reduced hunger. Most of the GMO corn and soya is however not going to feed people, it is going to feed cars as biofuel, it is going as cattle feed to torture animals in factory farms. Currently, the US uses 30% of its corn for biofuel. This only substitutes 1% of fossil fuel. If all US corn were to be used for biofuel, it would only substitute 7% of fossil fuel. A 100% substitution implies a land grab in poorer countries to grow the remaining 93% biofuel. Land grab uproots peasants and creates hunger.

Another myth is that small farms are inefficient and have low productivity and therefore small farmers shall disappear. This too is false. Small farms produce more food than large farms. As the former Indian Prime Minister Charan Singh said, 'Agriculture being a life process, in actual practice, under given conditions, yields per acre decline as the size of a farm increases (in other words, as the application of human labour and supervision per acre decrease). The above results are well-nigh universal: output per acre of investment is higher on small farms than on large farms. Thus, if a crowded, capital-scarce country like India has a choice between a single 100 acre farm, and forty 2.5 acre farms, the capital cost to the national economy will be less if the country chooses the small farms.'

A third myth is that industrial monocultures produce more food, and therefore biodiversity must disappear. Navdanya's work over the last 25 years has shown that biodiverse organic farming produces more food and nutrition than chemical monocultures. Our report *Health per Acre: Organic Solutions for Hunger and Malnutrition* shows that two Indias could be fed by biodiversity intensification and ecological intensification of food production. The dominant paradigm of industrial agriculture (called the Green Revolution and the second Green Revolution when GMO seeds are used) and globalized trade in food has pushed India into two deep crises.

The first is the agrarian crisis. High external input agriculture with the high costs of chemicals and non-renewable patented seed is pushing farmers into debt; more than 250,000 farmers have committed suicide. Most suicides are in the cotton belt, and most cotton seed is now owned and controlled by Monsanto. The second deep crisis is that of food and malnutrition. India, which has high economic growth rates, has also emerged as the capital of hunger. Every fourth Indian is hungry, every third Indian woman suffers from malnutrition, and every second child is severely malnourished. Two million children are dying of hunger every year for lack of food in India. Children who *are* eating are also suffering from malnutrition because India is seen as the biggest market by the junk food and processed food industry; 25% of the school-going children in cities like Delhi are now obese. India is the capital of diabetes because of the adoption of industrial food. Globally, while a billion people are hungry, two billion are suffering from diseases of obesity and diabetes.

No farmer should commit suicide. No child should die of hunger. No one should be sick because of food.

Navdanya's *Seed to Table* Experience in Delhi and Mumbai

We are at a watershed for human evolution: either we carry on mindlessly and jeopardize humanity's survival on this planet or we transform, recognize the reverence we owe to Mother Earth and adopt or rather revert to a sustainable and renewable way of agriculture that will be based on principles of equity, i.e., Food for All. We naturally believe in the second option, an option for which we have in fact been working for 25 years now. Gandhi said that it is to village India and to the strength of women that we will owe our fulfilment.

At Navdanya we have proactively started sowing the *Seeds of Freedom from Insecurity*, and creating *Gardens of Hope*, both at the rural and urban levels. Navdanya's *Asha Ke Beej, Asha Ke Chaman* (*Seeds of Hope, Gardens of Hope*) is a programme that offers a pragmatic and proactive solution in response to the deep food insecurity that is prevailing. Recognizing that as citizens we have the responsibility of taking actions when political will is non-existent, the *Gardens of Hope* programme partners with various stakeholders such as women, schools, and organizations at the grassroots level to help them create kitchen gardens, using open pollinated varieties of vegetable seeds, thus also countering the seed monopoly of the seed giants.

From *Seed to Table*, Navdanya protects and rebuilds both natural and social capital. The first link in the *Seed to Table* chain is our women-run community seed banks. We have started more than 66 community seed banks where we conserve and distribute seeds of 'forgotten foods' like the millets, seeds of climatic resilient crops, seeds of nutritious foods. This is reversing the erosion of seed, monopolies on seed, and the dominance of monocultures of four commodities: corn, soya, canola and cotton. Our *Seeds of Hope* are making seeds available in regions where lack of seed has made farmers dependent on patented seed with royalty payments. Our second link in the food chain is to join the seed and the soil in sustainable production through biodiverse organic farming. We have reached 500,000 farmers to practice an agriculture that protects the earth, rebuilds soil, enhances food production and increases rural incomes. We call our farmers co-creators, since they work *with* the earth, not against her. Since the web of life is a food web, we first think of feeding the millions of soil organisms. Since rural communities who produce our food also have a right to food, we ensure that every farming family grows enough food for their own nutritional needs. Since every person has a fundamental right to eat well and get healthy food, we link the rural areas to the cities through organic fair trade. We call our urban members co-producers, because in choosing biodiverse organic food, they are becoming partners with farmers in the act of producing good food. Navdanya has four retail outlets in Delhi and one in Mumbai. We run an organic café, where people can taste forgotten foods. But cities can be producers too. That is why we have started *Gardens of Hope* with schools. In gardening, every child becomes a potential farmer, a child of the earth, a creator. In a workshop-based programme students are initiated to the concept of *Vasudhaiva Kutumbakam,* which has a strong resonance with the movement to ensure the rights of Mother Earth; they are also motivated to reflect upon the food choices they make and their impact upon Mother Earth, farming communities, their well-being and various related topics. Since children are future decision makers, sowing the seeds of hope in their minds is a meaningful step towards working for food safety, food security, and food sovereignty.

At the grassroots level, the examples from Vidarbha illustrate how this programme operates. Since women were and are traditionally the keepers of seeds, Navdanya just consolidated or revived the practice. Women farmers create a *parasbaugh* or a kitchen garden in a space where vegetables, fruit trees, herbs and medicinal plants are intercropped. These gardens are a living example of biodiversity. There is food growing all year round using resources like gray water and compost from the kitchen garden; this ensures food and nutrition. It has an added advantage of creating a cool microclimate in the scorching heat of Vidarbha. The surplus is bartered with the neigh-bouring households. It can also be collected on an appointed day from each kitchen garden and sold at the weekly market, giving people some extra cash. A portion is selected and left to go to seed. After the fruit or vegetable is matured, it is harvested and dried appropriately. The women keep some seed for the next season and a portion is given to replenish the seed bank. Navdanya provides the women with seeds to plant these *parasbaughs*. This process has helped women in the area of Vidarbha to become providers of seed and food. There are 30 such functional *parasbaughs* in five villages of the Dhamangaon Taluka in West India.

Through our Mahila Anna Swaraj programme, which puts food safety, food security and food sovereignty back into women's hands, we revalidate women's generations-old knowledge and food wisdom to provide safe and nurturing food to our cities. Within this scheme, women in the rural areas organize themselves as a *samooh* or self-help group and artisanally process a range of products such as pickles, *vadis* (dried lentil dumplings), *papads* (thin crisp lentil flour bread with different flavourings).

These products, which are unique not only because of their gentle processing and light carbon footprints but also because of their authentic and distinctive taste, are then sold from the shelves of our direct marketing outlets.

At the urban level, what are the solutions available to the food issues with which we are plagued? Here too, taking responsibility as a civil society to ensure food safety, food security and food sovereignty is the key. In Mumbai, inspired by Navdanya's sustainable and ecological agricultural practice, Ubai, a young chef, has initiated Mumbai Organic Farmers and Consumers Association (MOFCA), a collective of 12 farmers. MOFCA has come up with a scheme called Hari Bhari Tokri, which offers consumers a basket of fresh veggies, a weekly supply sourced from farms within a radius of 150 km from Mumbai. Under the scheme one partners with a MOFCA farmer for an entire growing season (usually 3-4 months) by paying a deposit. For the first time, consumers are able to connect with the farmers, understand how and where the food that they consume comes from. By having a predetermined number of consumers to grow for, farmers are able to plan their growing cycle in advance. The consumer is assured of quality, without intermediaries, at reasonable prices that are not subject to economic fluctuations or false scarcity.

The Gandhian Concept of Sarvodaya

Looking back at all these initiatives, what comes out very clearly is that the too often quoted, less often followed Gandhian way 'Be the change you want to see', is the only way. It all starts with Swaraj, which means sovereignty of course, but which etymologically means 'Rule over yourself' or in other words: self-discipline. Unless each one decides individually to commit to create a more food secure earth, it is not going to happen. Then, the concept of Swadeshi, where we start in a decentralized manner, at the local level, before reaching to wider circles, is an important element to ensure both food security and political stability, because just like the Seed, Bija, which is put in the soil to grow upwards, so too a stable and meaningful governance must start from the grassroots and then reach the global arena. Here we have the model of Jaiv Panchayats, where at the level of the village people commit to safeguarding their traditional knowledge and heritage and alerting the powers that be whenever there is a default. The Gandhian concept of Sarvodaya, well-being for all, is just as crucial to the making of a food secure world. Unless the food security, food safety and food sovereignty of each and every living being are catered for, the eternal city-village tensions will continue. The village can feed the city but in return the city has to be respectful of the 3 S's of food. And lastly, Satyagraha, abiding by the truth with integrity in all that we do is just as crucial as the other Gandhian concepts. This is why Navdanya organizes Bija Satyagraha to protest unfair seed laws and monopolies or stands by with all sectors of society to protest all manner of takeovers such as that of land, as in the case of Niamgiri and Posco.

By 2050, Navdanya's innovations will be even more relevant than today. Industrial agriculture is 40% of the climate problem, 75% of the biodiversity erosion problem, 70% of the water problem, 70% of the public health and malnutrition problem, including both hunger and obesity. As India urbanizes, these concerns will deepen, not disappear. We will need to grow more nutritious food while using less water and consuming more biodiversity, rebuilding soil, reducing climate impact. Increasing health per acre while reducing our ecologic footprint is the challenge of the future. And that is the challenge we are addressing creatively and effectively.

Navadanya, the movement I launched, was and continues to be inspired by Gandhi and it would not be a cliché to end by saying we must all 'Be the change we seek to see'. We have a saying in India 'boond boond se sagar banta hai'; it means: every drop contributes to the making of the ocean; so let us each contribute to bring about a sea of change.

Arctic Food Network

The Architects / Urbanists
Lola Sheppard and
Mason White / Lateral Office

The Canadian architects and urban planners Lola Sheppard and Mason White of Lateral Office take up the challenge to develop a modest, small-scale infrastructure for the Inuit in the Canadian North. Their culture and livelihood is seriously jeopardized by changing climatological conditions, increasing exploitation of natural resources and imported southern models of language, food and culture.

see images on page 118-119

The myth of the Canadian North is tied to its unique geography – a territory vast, sparsely populated, fragile and sublime. Yet with a quarter of the globe's undiscovered energy resources and dramatically changing climatological conditions, the circum-polar region has become a site of economic and development speculation. In the 2006 Census, Canada's three northern territories – Yukon, Northwest Territories, and Nunavut – posted a combined population of over 100,000 people for the first time in Canadian history and Nunavut continues to significantly exceed Canada's average population growth rate. Some 33,000 people (84% Inuit) live dispersed across approximately 23 communities. Furthermore, populations in the North are remarkably young, adding to the growth rate. Yet with this urgency to expand, there is little vision of growth beyond economic expediency and efficiency, and the people here have typically imported southern models – be it of language, food, housing or education. Development in the North has been intimately tied to the construction of infrastructure, yet these projects are rarely conceived with a long-term, holistic vision. The Canadian North's unique combination of climate, culture and geography has produced complicated settlements, infrastructures and socio-political negotiations. The question emerges, how might future developments participate in cultivating and perpetuating ecosystems and local cultures, rather than threatening them?

Challenges & Food Security

Some of the greatest challenges facing northern communities are physical isolation, economic marginalization, youth disenfranchisement, and loss of traditional knowledge. The younger generations of Inuit find themselves caught between traditional and contemporary cultures. To add to this, changes in lifestyle have produced health issues; over-crowding in houses has contributed to high levels of tuberculosis, while changes in diet have increased obesity and diabetes levels.

The traditional Inuit diet, which is centred on hunting and fishing, has been slowly compromised by an influx of southern manufactured food products. Both north and south are coping with the health impacts of this diet; but it is amplified in the north, due to the high cost of shipping fresh produce and healthier, perishable goods to radically dispersed and remote northern communities. A typical food basket in Nunavut is twice the cost ($275-322) of the same food basket in southern Canada[1] while at the same time levels of unemployment are much higher in the North – in some communities, as much as a third of families are on social assistance. As a result, the 2006 Aboriginal Peoples Survey showed that in Nunavut, nearly forty per cent of Inuit children aged 6 to 14 had experienced hunger at some point in a given month because the family had run out of food or money to buy food.[2]

Nunavut, like much of the Arctic, is also suffering from dramatic changes in climate. Elders, who traditionally have an uncanny knowledge of the land, are less and less able to 'read' it, due to the unpredictability of weather patterns and ice formation. As a result, there is increasing need to rely on new technologies. The Inuit have adapted to climate change by finding new – and often longer – routes to reach their hunting areas and relying on new technologies such as global positioning system devices and satellite phones to enhance safety. They use all-terrain vehicles when there is not enough snow on the ground to support snowmobiles and they now hunt from boats instead of on less stable sea ice. But the extra fuel needed for these forms of transportation has made hunting more expensive.[3]

Food Culture

The role of hunting and fishing in the North, but also food storage and preparation, has been central to collective life, because of the constant challenges of traditionally sourcing food. As a population that was nomadic until the 1950s, the Inuit would move seasonally to hunt, fish and collect berries. Even today, the tradition of going out into the land to hunt continues (as partial subsistence living), and many northerners have cabins 'out on the land'. There is also a strong tradition of sharing food amongst families, and even amongst communities, in times of need. As a consequence, food is deeply embedded in the Inuit people's relationship to the land, to mobility, and culture.

Arctic Food Network (AFN) proposes a snowmobile-accessed, regional network of hunting cabins, arctic farms and camp hubs. The AFN encircles the large body of the Foxe Basin in Nunavut, Canada, home to a richly diverse wildlife, along the coast of Baffin Island and some 11,000 Nunavummiut. The project takes advantage of an existing network of snowmobile trails, the only form of ground connection between the eleven disconnected Inuit communities of Baffin Island. A regional study on mobility, food security, and health in the region led to the pursuit of a network of small structures that acknowledge the Inuit tradition of temporary enclosure in a cold climate. The project seeks to recover local food traditions, engage an increasing and youthful population in northern settlements, but also potentially offer a future exportable economy.

Northern Ecologies

Each of the hubs along the AFN opportunistically negotiates its local ecosystems, emergent biological potentials, and its proximity to communities. The hubs are proposed to be distributed at 160 km intervals, a reasonable distance which can be travelled by snow-mobile. Hubs occupy varied sites: inland, water/ice, or coastal conditions, and each of these locations is selected for its access to a specific harvestable food product.

Despite a perception of arctic barrenness, there is a rich diversity of northern ecologies. The main sources of traditional food for the Inuit include meats such as caribou and polar bear, sea mammals such as walrus, narwhal and seal, arctic char, shellfish such as shrimp, scallops and mussels and seasonal berries. Meat is traditionally eaten raw or smoked, as this retains much more of its nutritional value, and animals are eaten in their entirety – virtually nothing is left to waste. A territorial map of regions of productive overlaps of species helped determine potential locations for the AFN hubs.

Cabins, Meshes and Poles

The network of hubs is comprised of cabins, sheds, meshes, and poles, which refer to a set of uniquely integrated elements merging architecture, landscape, and technology. These elements assist in negotiating the harsh dark winters and treeless landscape of the Canadian North. They play off an existing tradition of seasonal buildings which support local food gathering: fishing sheds, overnight hunting cabins, community freezers, and northern greenhouses. Cabins consist of ice fishing shacks, smoking shacks, food preparation spaces, and overnight cabins for hunters. Sheds consist of seasonal greenhouses, root vegetable vaults, underground freezers. Meshes lain horizontally can grow kelp and seaweed for harvesting, or put up vertically can be used for drying fish and meat. Poles are used for way-finding; either as lighting in the winter darkness, or as telecommunications towers.

Conceived as a kit of parts, the project is intended to be adaptable, deployed incrementally, and cost-efficient, while providing a network of modest shelters that serve mobility in harsh climate, support social networks, and strengthen traditional learning. Because of this flexibility, the focus of different sites can adapt to needs: some might focus more on hunting or fishing cabins, others more on harvestable arctic produce.

New Northern Vernaculars

The *Arctic Food Network* project is equal parts regional agriculture, seasonal camps, data transmission centres, and ecological management stations. Hubs along the snowmobile trails might be just one shelter or several, depending on the needs of the adjacent communities, and intensity of use. In addition to providing a secure food and travel network, AFN seeks to merge new technologies with traditional practices to support an emergent 21st-century economy. Construction of the shelters negotiates traditional and contemporary construction techniques. Some walls would be relatively open, allowing air to flow in the summer and snow to be packed into the wall in the winter. Inversely, research into photovoltaic cells embedded in the metal skin could support light and data transmitters in poles for additional safety.

The *Arctic Food Network* began as a design research project looking at the roles and opportunities for modest, small-scale infrastructure in the Canadian North to serve as a cultural and economic catalyst for remote communities. The work was initially funded by the Canada Council for Arts Prix de Rome award. The project is on-going, and current development is being funded by the Holcim Foundation for Sustainable Construction. Lateral Office is now in discussions with numerous government ministries in Nunavut to move the project forward. The next phase will be to develop institutional and community partners to discuss in greater detail the needs of individual communities, and to develop prototypes for specific locations.

Extrinsic Architectures

The Arctic Food Network project and much of Lateral's work seek to reposition the role of the architect away from simply problem solver or designer, toward a cultural, environmental and spatial detective; one who brings to light the influences (geographic, economic, and cultural) at work within a site-specific climate and geography, and looks for synergies between issues and opportunities. The role of the architect is understood as operating across and in between the disciplines of architecture, landscape architecture, ecology, geographer, regional planner, and technologist. The work also advocates an extrinsic architecture, one capable of embracing its larger contexts of geography, economics and ecology; and is adept at recognizing the fluidity of boundaries, and the multiple forces operating within a site.

In the North, it is incumbent upon an extrinsic architecture to engage the social challenges facing local populations, however modestly. The *Arctic Food Network* attempts to provide social infrastructure by which communities could return to, and expand, traditions of hunting or food sharing. Some of the components of the project build upon existing traditions (such as the fishing cabins and community freezers) while others (such as the greenhouses, the meat smoking cabins, the water-borne shed, or telecommunications towers) attempt to build community capacity and productivity by making traditional hunting more accessible or efficient. In setting up a more legible and distributed network of hubs, the projects also hopes to re-engage youth in traditional hunting practices. While the specific components of *the Arctic Food Network* are uniquely geared to their geography, the notion of incremental, small-scale interventions to encourage local food production is entirely transferable and would no doubt thrive.

Despite the extensive research on issues of Northern culture, identity, autonomy, etc, there has been virtually no discussion of the role of architecture. *The Arctic Food Network* posits, as a departing point, the critical role that architecture and infrastructure will play shaping northern identity – not simply in imagining new northern vernaculars that bridge traditional and contemporary practices, but more significantly, in imagining new roles and programmes for social infrastructure – adapted to the unique geography and culture of the Arctic. The project asks the question of how can remote communities network themselves, spatially and operationally, in order to share and expand social and cultural resources? And what new building and urban typologies are required to enable such networking of resources? In a landscape of extremes that oscillates between freeze and thaw, dark and light, accessible and inaccessible, *Arctic Food Network* looks at the roles and challenges of the public realm, landscape and infrastructure in the North, and envisions a model of architecture and infrastructure that is in geographically scalable, environmentally responsive, and programmatically multi-valent.

Food Prices Increase Towards 2050

Projected changes of the global food prices towards 2050 for two biofuel expansion scenarios, compared to the baseline scenario of conservative biofuel development. The biofuel expansion scenario assumes that current biofuel plans are executed, while the drastic biofuel expansion scenario is based on a more rapid growth of biofuel production.

Source: M.W. Rosegrant, M. Ewing, S. Msangi and T. Zhu, *Bioenergy and global food situation until 2020/2050* (Washington DC, Berlin: Springer, 2008)

- **Biofuel expansion (price changes in %)**
- **Drastic biofuel expansion (price changes in %)**

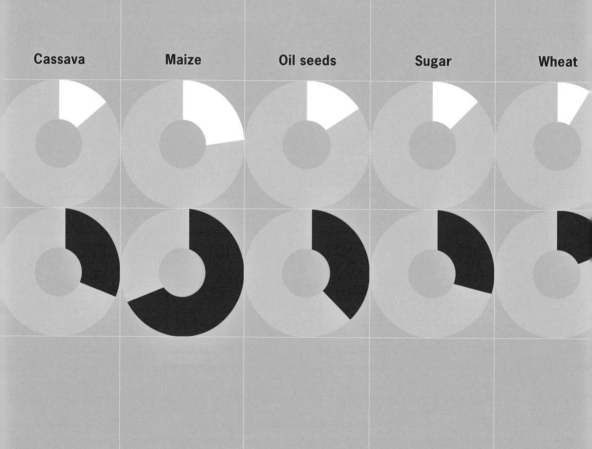

| Cassava | Maize | Oil seeds | Sugar | Wheat |

Ecological Debt Towards 2050: A Need for Multiple Earths

Projections of the demand that development of humanity will pose on the Earth. This scenario takes into account human demand on agriculture, forests, fish, and built-up land under increasing farm yields.

Source:B. Erwing, S. Goldfinger, M. Wackernagel, et al, *The ecological footprint atlas* (Oakland: Global footprint network, 2008)

One world

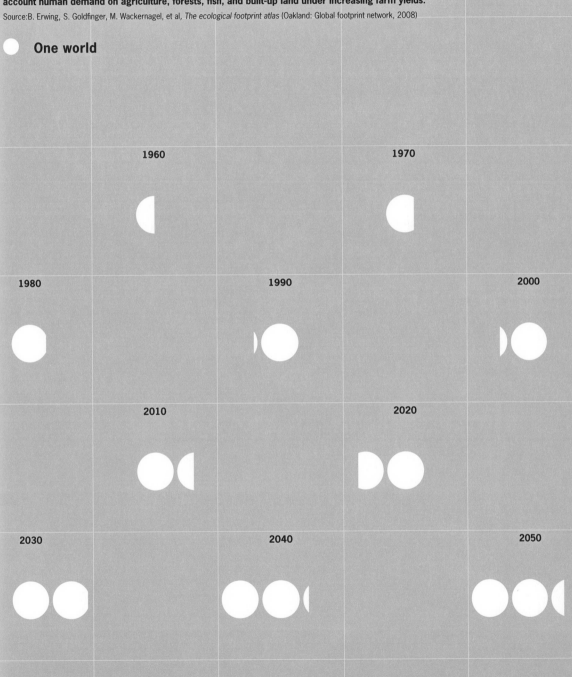

Food Culture

page 201
The British speculative designer James King examines new shapes, textures and flavours of in-vitro meat in his project *Dressing the Meat of Tomorrow*. Scouring the countryside for the most beautiful cows, pigs, chicken and other livestock, King scans the animals from head to toe, seeking cross-sectional moulds that will create new authentic forms of food, without the cruelty of slaughtering the animal.

page 202-203
'What's on family dinner tables around the globe?', American photographer Peter Menzel and writer Faith D'Alusio asked during their trip to 24 countries and 30 families. The photos portray the families at home, at the market or in their community with their weekly food purchases. All portraits are published in the book *Hungry Planet. What the World Eats*, 2007.

Photo: Peter Menzel and Faith D'Alusio. Source: Hollandse Hoogte

page 202 top
The Namgay family of Shingkhey Village, Bhutan. Food expenditure for one week: $5.03.

page 202 bottom
The Casales family in the open-air living room of their home in Cuernavaca, Mexico. Food expenditure for one week: $189.09.

page 203 top
The Ayme family in their kitchen house in Tingo, Ecuador. Food expenditure for one week: $31.55.

page 203 bottom
The Aboubakar family of Darfur province, Sudan, in front of their tent in the Breidjing Refugee Camp, in eastern Chad. Food expenditure for one week: $ 1.23.

page 204 top + bottom
A visualization of the CO_2 emissions of two different kinds of breakfast in 2007 by the British artist's network Extreme Green Guerillas. Starting with the question 'What would an extreme green food look like?' they consider eating a road-kill diet, but decide that it is not appealing enough. Modifying urban vermin with gourmet animals could be a solution.

Photo: Yumiko Tanaka. Source: Extreme Green Guerillas

page 205
With culinary specialties as the '15 inch pure beef frankfurter Home Wrecker' and the 'Big Bad Bubba Burger', the restaurant Hillbilly Hot Dogs in Huntington, West Virginia, was the perfect location for Naked Chef Jamie Oliver's new show on the eating habits of the residents in the unhealthiest town in the US.

Photo: Mark Peterson/Redux, 2009. Source: Hollandse Hoogte

page 2006-207
Food stall on the market of Jamaa el Fna, the main square in Marrakech, Morocco.

Photo and source: Yvonne Wassink, 2009

page 208 top
Muslims in Lahore, Pakistan gather for 'iftar', the evening meal to break their fast on the first day of the holy fasting month Ramadan. From dawn to dusk people refrain from eating, drinking, smoking and sex. It is a time for reflection, devotion, self-control and charity. At the end of the month Muslims are obligated to share their blessings by feeding the poor.

Photo: K.M. Chaudary, 2011. Source: Reporters/AP

page 208 bottom
Polish Jews gather together in Warsaw for Passover Seder, a ritual feast that marks the beginning of the Jewish holiday of Passover. The Seder involves the retelling of the story of the Israelites' escape from slavery in ancient Egypt and includes the drinking of four cups of wine, eating matza and the six symbolic foods placed on the Seder Plate.

Photo: Tomasz Tomaszewski, 1986. Source: National Geographic/Getty Images

Conventional breakfast costs 2377kg CO2 emission in total.

Fair trade coffee:

1450 kg CO2 emission

Peru · London
More than 5000 miles by airplane.

Italian salad:

260 kg CO2 emission

Rome · London
897 miles by airplane

Organic bacon:

308 kg CO2 emission

Denmark · London
1063 miles by airplane

Organic tomato:

227 kg emission

Madrid · London
784 miles by airplane

Free range eggs:

144 kg CO2 emission

Scotland · London
400 miles in a petrol car

Extreme green guerrilla's breakfast costs 0kg emission in total.

Herbal tea:

0kg CO2 emission

Picked up from garden

Piguail meat:

0kg emission

anywhere around house

No feeding needed

lawn salad:

0kg CO2 emission

Picked up from local park

Piguail eggs:

0kg CO2 emission

Local park

Meat from roadkill:

0kg CO2 emission

Nearest road

No feeding needed.

Mushroom:

0kg CO2 emission

Local park

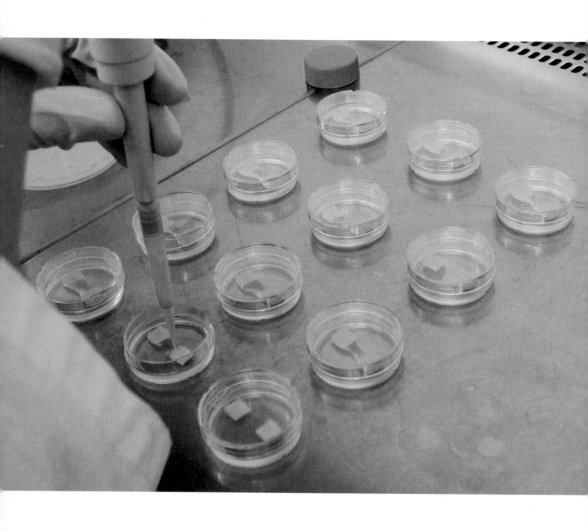

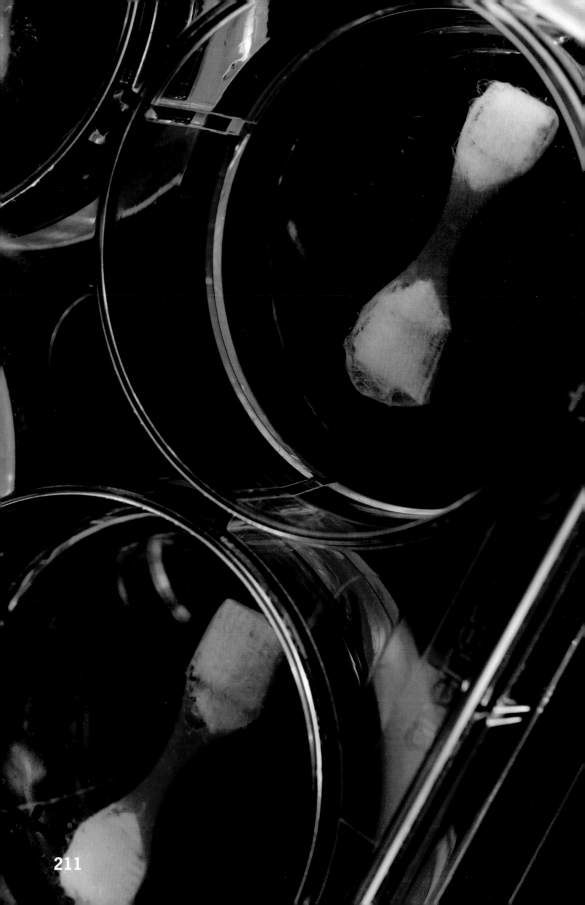

Tlaxcales

Huauhtzontles

Elotes

MICHMOLE
ROJO

Atole de masa
(Maíz remojado)

Conserva de Tejocotes

Tortillas

Ahuautle

Tacatitos

Atole de amaranto

OCOTE

TLACOYOS

213

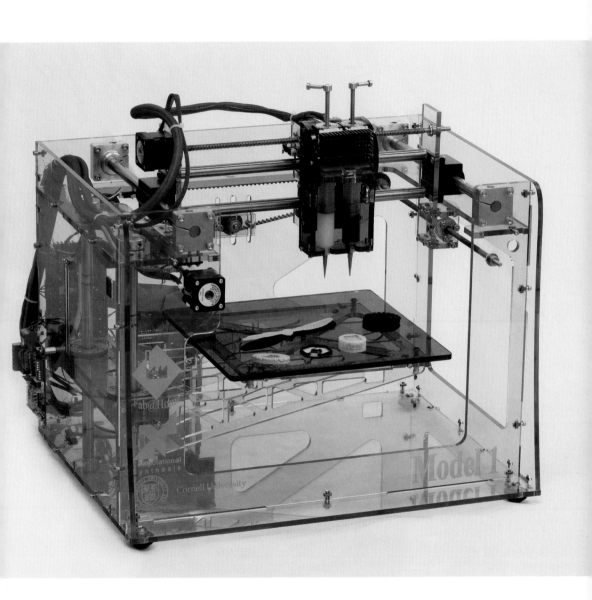

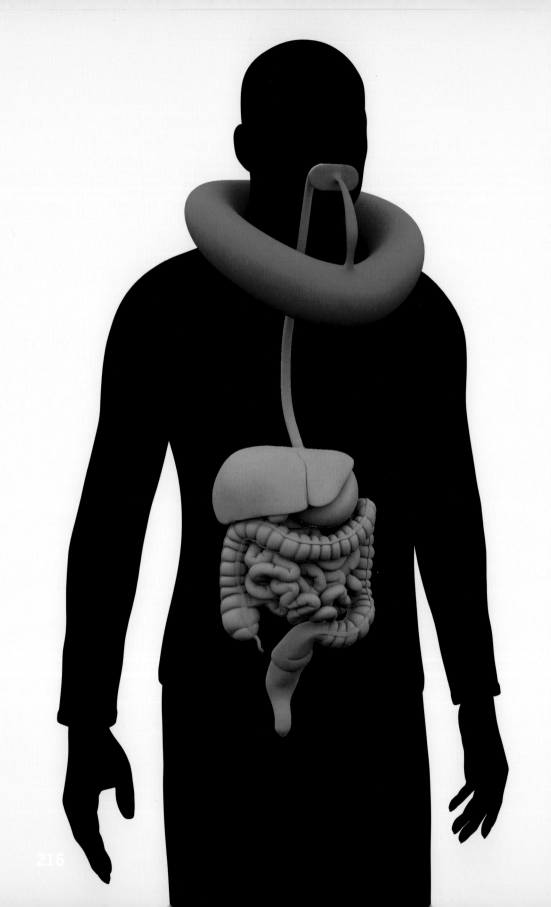

elBulli was a 3-star Michelin restaurant run by chef Ferran Adrià near the town of Roses in Catalonia, Spain. Adrià described his way of cooking with the term 'deconstructivist': radical experiments with the physical and chemical transformations of ingredients. Guests had to book years in advance to experience food that engaged all the senses as well as the mind, according to the great chef. In July 2011 elBulli closed, but it will open in 2014 as the elBullifoundation, an archive and brainstorming centre dedicated to culinary creativity.

Photo: Charles Haynes, 2007. Source: elBulli

Cultured meat or in-vitro meat could be the answer to the world's increasing hunger for meat. Scientists from the universities in Maastricht and Eindhoven in the Netherlands experiment with lab-grown meat and muscles, using stem cells from mice and other leftover animal material from the slaughterhouse. Though not very substantial or tasty yet, scientists are confident that the first man-made hamburger will be ready within a year.

Photo: Carlijn Bouten, 2011. Source: TUe (Eindhoven University of Technology)

Food offerings for ancestors on shrines near the historic Buddhist temple One Pillar Pagoda in Hanoi, Vietnam. In Vietnam people traditionally celebrate the anniversaries of the death of loved ones, but also offer food to ancestors in traditional or religious celebrations, or on more mundane occasions like the starting of a new business.

Photo and source: Karin Kaldenhoven, 2011

Every year on 2 November, people in Mexico celebrate the Day of the Dead, or All Souls Day. Believing that death is a transition of one life to another, the Day of the Dead is a colourful celebration of life. Altars honouring the deceased are decorated with marigolds and present the favourite food and beverages of the departed.

Photo: Edgar Xolot, 2011. Source: LatinContent/Getty Images

The crew of the NASA 2003 Expedition 7, consisting of commander Yuri Malenchenko and Flight Engineer Ed Lu, share a meal in the Zvezda Service Module. In the background is a potable water heater and attached to the edge of the table are various utensils.

Photo and source: NASA, Space Food Fact Sheets

There are still some problems to be solved, but the team of scientists and engineers at Cornell University's Computational Synthesis Lab are working hard to bring the 3-D food printer to the home environment. The edible inks will be able to print everything from apple pies and cookies to a turkey dinner.

Photo: Floris van Breugel/Fab@Home, 2011. Source: FAB@Home

British design studio Dunne & Raby's *Designs for an overpopulated planet: the Foragers* from 2009 is a bottom-up approach to current and future food shortages. Using synthetic biology to create 'microbial stomach bacteria', Dunne & Raby maximize the nutritional value of vegetation and other material found in the urban environment. The new urban foragers take their fate into their own hands.

Render and source: Dunne & Raby, 2009

Women's Quest to Secure Food in Post-Conflict East Africa

The Women's Rights Advocate
Gaynor Paradza

Gaynor Paradza, the Zimbabwean senior researcher of
land and agrarian reform at the Institute for Poverty, Land
and Agrarian Studies (PLAAS) in South Africa, describes
women's quest for food in post-conflict East Africa.
Surprisingly, destabilization provides opportunities to
strengthen policy revision in the interest of women, who
contribute to 70% of Africa's food production and 80-90%
of food processing, storage and transport.

Experts report that women in Africa contribute 70% of food production. They also account for nearly half of all farm labour and 80-90% of food processing, storage and transport.[1] The majority of the women depend on land to perform these roles. Although the developing world houses the majority of the poor, people living in conflict or post-conflict situations are relatively more vulnerable. This vulnerability is induced by limited capacity, inefficiency of food production systems and weak and ineffective governance institutions. Women have the primary responsibility for procuring food. In order to fulfil this subsistence role, this segment of the population needs secure access to fertile land, inputs and labour. The dominant practise in land held under customary tenure in Africa is that women have derived rights to land, i.e. they negotiate land through a male relative and/or husband. This renders women's land rights fragile and subject to constant negotiation. Conflict–induced displacement undermines access to land and limits people's capacity to produce their own food. This article offers a short reflection on the position of women farmers in post-conflict situations and concludes by recommending the measures that need to be taken to secure women's access to land.

Background

Women in the developing world are responsible for food production. This is a socially ascribed role that complements their task of reproduction, and care for the disabled and ill. In a peace situation this means growing and foraging for food from the land and forest and going to markets. Markets really function in times of peace. Land is the primary asset for generating a livelihood and social security. In exacerbated conflict, people lose jobs and their means of earning an income. This leads to an increased reliance on self-production. Women become increasingly marginalized as populations are displaced and adult men are lost to war. The women's capacity to grow food is undermined by lack of land, lack of security and stability, labour and inputs. There is also pressure from internal conflict: for example, although the peace accord has been signed in Sudan, ethnic conflict continues among the estimated 65 ethnic groups. This perpetuates instability and food insecurity in the marginalized areas. East Africa has been a volatile enclave in the latter part of the last century. Rwanda, Somalia, the Sudan, and parts of Kenya have endured sustained conflict. The violence in Rwanda has been attributed to ethnic tensions and political competition for power and control of land and other natural resources.[2] In the Sudan, conflict was precipitated by the struggle for self-determination. The Ugandans were rebelling against bad governance, while in Kenya the causes are less well-defined.[3] The violence that is characteristic of these conflicts has led to the destruction of social structures and infrastructure, and mass displacement, forcing people to abandon their land. The destruction of social structures for negotiating access to resources undermines women's land access, which in most cases is already fragile during peace times as it has to be constantly renegotiated. This is not to generalize the experiences of women in the region but to highlight the specific ways in which women's experience of conflict specifically undermines their land access and food providing role.

The Situation of Women Farmers in a Post-conflict Situation

Women in a post-conflict situation are food insecure and face the challenges of trying to secure land without men in a male-biased society. In South Sudan, by the end of the war, 35% of the women had become widow while 68% of the domestic units were headed by women.[4] During the war in Rwanda, hundreds of thousands of women were forced to flee their communities. After the war, many women returned to their own and other communities, without husbands or male relatives, only to discover that the land that they hoped to claim was occupied by other refugees.[5] The 2007 electoral violence in Kenya displaced more than 800,000 people. The Kenyan government initially provided tents and established holding camps for the displaced. The government later closed the holding camps and gave displaced people money to return to their homes. The men collected the money as head of households and abandoned the women in the holding camps.[6] In addition to food insecurity, the women on their own have an increased burden of care as a result of war injuries and are more reliant on basic survival food procurement strategies like foraging. The destruction and displacement caused by war reduces women's capacity to fulfil their primary food procuring role. The structures that facilitate access to land include male heads of households and customary institutions and practices that safeguard women's access to land. The women who are more reliant on customary land have more difficulty in enforcing their claims in a post-conflict situation. This is because customary institutions set aside practices that protect women. Experiences from Rwanda illustrate that although conflicts disrupt women's food provisioning, the destabilization provides opportunities to challenge existing norms and strengthen gender equality and policy revision in the interest of women.

As returning refugees compete for land and rights to natural resource, there is an increase in competing claims. Women's derived land rights tend to be overlooked. The existence of weak land governance, policy administration and information management systems and the absence of women from strategic decision making structures exacerbate the situation. In Rwanda women involved in land disputes faced an average of at least one year to get their case resolved by institutions dealing in land law, and usually abandoned the case. In some cases, the institutions might demand a bribe from those seeking a service, which further marginalizes women.[7] Women in post-conflict situations have difficulties securing food and initially a large number of them depend on food aid if this is available. Even then, this is usually not enough to meet their domestic family requirements. Others try self-provision by growing their own food. This is only possible if they have access to land and inputs, and secure land. Increasingly though the women with limited access to livelihood resources turn to risky coping strategies such as prostitution to secure money to buy food. Others rely on their own limited resources like labour to negotiate food access. The returns from such transactions are usually inadequate to meet the needs of the woman and her family as host communities usually exploit the vulnerable refugees.

Strategies to Secure Women's Access to Land: Case Studies from Kenya and Rwanda

The experience in Kenya, where people lost their land during electoral violence, highlights an effective strategy that was used by internally displaced people with the assistance of a non-governmental organization, Kenya Land Alliance, to secure land for food production in the face of limited government support and intervention. The Kenyan Land Alliance assisted internally displaced people who were housed in a camp on the edge of an urban settlement in securing land. The community – consisting mostly of women who had been abandoned by their men in the refugee holding camps – pooled the money that the government had given them to return to their homes and negotiated access to 19 acres of land. The land was divided into individual portions and each domestic unit was allocated a portion. All men and women were treated the same. The community initially produced food for their subsistence. Over time they started to produce crops to sell to the surrounding community. The former internally displaced people (IDP) used the proceeds to hire land surveyors and they secured a group title deed. This secured their tenure on the piece of land and enabled women who would otherwise have difficulty in securing land and/or reasserting their land rights in a post-conflict situation.[8]

During the post–conflict land redistribution the government of Rwanda committed itself to addressing all types of discrimination, including that based on gender. This was in recognition of the critical role that women play in food procurement and the fact that the majority of surviving households were headed by women. The President took the lead by making policy statements that committed the government, and the cabinet received training in gender issues, which facilitated the community's acceptance of and support for the focus on women's land rights. There was an innovative law reform that awarded male and female children were equal land inheritance status. In some situations, villages for women and children only were established to provide land access for those women and children who for some reason had failed to re-establish a land claim after the conflict.[9]

What Action Should be Taken and by Whom to Secure Women's Access to Land

Although it is a challenge to secure women's land access in a post-conflict situation to enable them to produce food, it is not impossible. A review of success stories in East Africa has illustrated that political will is an important precondition for mobilizing resources and support for women's land access. The experiences from Kenya also illustrate how bottom-up initiatives and people's inventiveness can also facilitate women's land tenure security. This should be buttressed with gender responsive allocation of resources as was done in Rwanda.[10]

Governments should also invest in proactive initiatives aimed at reforming traditional practices and attitudes that undermine women's access to land. This includes community awareness campaigns, harnessing women's agency, adult literacy, succession planning and mainstreaming gender into educational programmes.[11]

Governments should provide clear guidelines to enable the displaced people to claim land. Institutions should have the capacity to administer both written and oral claims to land. As single women-headed households increase in conflict situations, governments should increase women's capacity to access land through the market and through government allocation, in order to reduce women's dependence on succession and inheritance and marriage, as inheritance and marital practices undermine women's access to land and perpetuate their dependence on male-dominated structures.[12] Registration of land in the name of a community or group is a strategy that can help women gain secure access to land without having to negotiate with gender-biased male-dominated institutions on an individual basis.

There is also a need to maintain stability to and good governance to ensure that people can rebuild their homes and re-establish their livelihoods in a post-conflict scenario. This should be done with a combination of government and non-governmental sectors, as governments in post-conflict situations often lack resources to secure and stabilize communities outside the urban areas where, unfortunately, the majority of the women are located. The strategy of government working effectively with funding agencies bore fruit in Rwanda, where multinational agencies played a role not only to fund the construction of shelter, but had opportunities to demonstrate effective innovations such as the construction of exclusive villages for women and children and the funding of support for programmes to provide gender responsive training for the president and the cabinet.[13]

Women can benefit from legal and extra-legal systems that provide them with autonomous land claims. This could be done through, for example, the establishment of sustainable models with investors that secure land, but allow women and communities to produce subsistence food. This can be done through increasing access to markets, providing assistance with equipment and infrastructure and provide labour-saving devices and farming equipment.

Experiences from Rwanda, Sudan and other post-conflict countries illustrate the need for massive financial and technical investments to enable institutions to function. The burden almost always exceeds the host government's capacity to provide. As the experience with the Kenyan Land Alliance shows, non-governmental organizations can complement the government. It is important for governments to accept the assistance of non-governmental and donor agencies who may have the requisite expertise, flexibility and resources to support the establishment of institutions and facilities that allow farmers to re-establish their livelihoods. Research by the International Land Coalition on women's land rights in East Africa showed that community-based interventions can not only complement government policies but also provide more effective means through which these policies can be implemented for the benefit of women. While state-led initiatives through law reform provide some leverage, the actual implementation and practice on the ground is better performed by local institutions that do not necessarily belong to the formal governance structures. The research illustrated how innovations by local institutions provide opportunities for interventions that address specific obstacles to women's land access in a particular location and context.[14]

Food self-procurement through subsistence farming, foraging and hunting is an important source of food for poor and marginalized people. Although women make up the majority of the poor and marginalized and food self-provisioning is a relatively accessible mechanism for securing food, it is conditional on secured access to land and forest produce. In order to secure the fragile rights and claims of women farmers, it is important that governments put in place mechanisms to monitor and protect women's land rights. This can be done through collaborative efforts between the state, local watchdog groups, research institutions and civil society organizations that work in the arenas of rights protection. It is important to look beyond urban bias, state law and pre-conflict systems to devise locally manageable responsive and secure land access mechanisms for women farmers.

Manifesto of Urban Cannibalism
(Amsterdam Declaration)

The Artists
Wietske Maas
and Matteo Pasquinelli

Urbanibalists Wietske Maas from the Netherlands and Matteo Pasquinelli from Italy evoke an image of the edible city in a hallucinatory trip through literature, philosophy, history and gastronomy. Theirs is a city of excess, an art of overgrowth. Buildings are liquid strata of minerals – just very slow.

We should never abandon the city in favour of a virgin territory.

There is no innocent state of nature to defend: cities are flourishing ecosystems in themselves, a true 'human participation in nature'.[1]

In fact, *nature builds no idea of nature*. The image of nature has always been an artefact of human civilization, a mark of its stage of evolution. Yet we remain unaware that this image is still the projection of our animal instincts and fears on the surrounding environment.

Any utopia of nature will always be the territorial gesture of a form of life.

'From the most ancient of times, from Neolithic and even Palaeolithic times, it is the town that invents agriculture'.[2] In the sixteenth century eastern Europe was converted into a vast countryside for western cities, and thereafter the 'new world' was forced into becoming countryside for the 'old world'.

If in the modern age 'Europe was beginning to devour, to digest the world',[3] urban cannibalism is the nemesis of late capitalism.

Urban cannibalism emerges from the biomorphic unconscious of the metropolis.

Innervated by flows of energy and matter, the urban landscape is alive. Hydraulic forces ebb and surge through a tangled skein of canals and sewers, water being one of the main metabolisms of the city.[4] But also buildings are liquid strata of minerals – just very slow.

About eight thousand years ago, the city was born as an exoskeleton of the human, an external remineralization of our internal bone structure to protect and guide the commerce of bodies in and beyond its walls.[5]

The apparently inorganic shell of the city is also part of an external geographical metabolism. Like our bones absorb calcium from rocks, Amsterdam was built 'on Norway', on the timber felled and shipped down along the Scandinavian fjords to build Dutch naval power.[6]

Enclosed by the town's walls, the promiscuous society of animals and humans was very conducive to epidemics. Plague and pox however were never passive inhabitants: bacteria and viruses invisibly 'redesigned' streets and houses, shaping also the form of institutions like hospitals and prisons.[7]

Any wall is populated and consumed by the invisible food chains of microbes and mould, where the border between organic and inorganic life blurs.

Buildings breathe and ferment. Architecture is the bunker of life.

Urban cannibalism is the art of overgrowth.

Instead of manicuring 'sustainable gardens', urban cannibalism celebrates the spontaneous surplus of the city's life. There are no interstices and no in-betweens: everything grows against everything else. The city is a place of excess.

It was Gilles Clement who mapped the *residues* of the city and disclosed the potentiality of the 'third landscape'. Urban cannibalism nurtures these 'biological corridors' that make species flourish, circulate and escape across both the *city of nature* and the *city of culture*.

Like at the time of the French Revolution, the third landscape refers to the revolt of the Third Estate against the old regime, and not to the Third World.[8] This landscape expresses neither power nor naked submission to power, but the common *potentia* of the soil – a telluric insurgency.

Urban cannibalism is the *third landscape of food* – instinctive ingredients that change the horizon of edibility, cutting to the core of culinary traditions and shovelling across the institutions of art. The whole city becomes a spontaneous *convivium*.

As with the siege of the Paris Commune, when communards ate the animals of the zoo and thereby engaged in a rebellious and joyful *expansion of the edible*.

'It was because we never had grammars, nor collections of old plants. And we never knew what urban, suburban, frontier and continental were. Lazy in the *mapamundi* of Brazil.'[9]

The reversal of frontiers into life. The city devouring itself.

Urban cannibalism does not recognise the Parliament of Things, nor any 'ecological institution' that fragments the city into abstract entities and binary relations.[10]

Life is a ternary movement far from equilibrium. 'We parasite each other and live among parasites', Michel Serres reminded us.

We inhabit a *natura naturans* – a never-ending chain of organisms cannibalizing each other right down to the invisible ones: 'The fruit spoils, the milk sours, the wine turns into vinegar, the vegetables rot, the stores of wheat are filled with rats and weevils. Everything ferments, everything rots. Everything changes.'[11]

Microorganisms take our dead body back to the soil. Putrefaction is still life.

The alliance with this kingdom of parasites and the rise of 'the civilization of yeast' made humanity win the first wars against noxious microbes. Yeast is the truly 'divine' agent that made the miracle of turning water into wine and gave us a new life. Greek gods knew that ambrosia, the first alcoholic drink of humankind, was the secret of immortality.

'Beer, wine, and bread, foods of fermentation, of bubbling, foods of decay, appeared as safeguards against death. These were our first great victories over parasites, our rivals... From the Olympians to the Last Supper, we have celebrated the victory to which we owe our life, the eternity of phylogenesis, and we celebrated it in its natural spot, the table.'[12]

'To feed is the most basic verb, the most fundamental, the most rooted. It expresses the primordial activity, the primary, basic function, the act 'I' engage in even before I am born or begin breathing. Because of it I belong to the earth forever. Like the smallest animal crawling in the dirt, like the smallest plant, I began by feeding myself.'[13]

Evolution itself started with an act of cannibalism and not by a simple genetic roulette. Bigger cells swallowed up organelles like mitochondria and so constituted higher forms of life that colonized this planet.[14]

All the life of the spirit, from philosophy to poetry, brings trace of this remote event, of this ancestral endosymbiosis. Inspiration is always an act of incorporation, as Novalis would say.

'All enjoyment, all taking in and assimilation, is eating, or rather: eating is nothing other than assimilation. All spiritual pleasure can be expressed through eating. In friendship, one really eats of the friend, or feeds on him. It is a genuine trope to substitute the body for the spirit – and, at a commemorative dinner for a friend, to enjoy, with bold, supersensual imagination, his flesh in every bite, and his blood in every gulp.'[15]

Eating an 'I', eating an eye. Incorporation – and not *sensation* – is the ultimate vehicle of the experience of the world. Centuries after Spinoza, we will still do not know 'what a body can do'.[16]

For ancient cultures it was common to unify mouth and spirit. In Latin *sapiens* literally meant the man with taste – the man with a sophisticated palate![17] The very corporeal taste of the mouth then passed to signify the incorporeal taste of the mind. But all science remains secretly a branch of *gastronomia*, the art of governing the stomach.

Ascending from the mouth, western civilisation grew further and extended from the organ of sight – the eye becoming the archetype of all spiritual and artistic activities for centuries.

In ancient Greece *theory* shared the same root as the word *theatre* and all its spectators. Today psychoanalysis is still promoting the voyeurism of the mind with all its family couches, *natures mortes* and political spectres.

No, the unconscious is not a theatre – but a mouth! Happy is the one who, like De Andrade, knows that taboos and traumas can be cannibalized...

Desire is a devouring, digesting, defecating machine. 'The *id* is at work everywhere... It breathes, it heats, it eats. It shits and fucks.' Deleuze and Guattari told us, though not vividly enough.[18]

It was religion which managed to subjugate the stomach into the crypto-cannibalistic ritual of the Christian communion. The 'ingestion of God' was introduced to exorcise the 'ingestion of the enemy' and clearly tame the social unrest of the urban cannibals.

Before becoming incorporeal, the spirit in medieval medicine was still a *spiritus animalis* circulating through the body. And looking carefully, cannibalistic appetites are found buried everywhere even in the foundations of the cathedral of the bourgeoisie: Hegel's philosophy.[19]

Today is the time to resuscitate the hidden demons of western culture. No longer the 'synthesis' or the 'becoming', but the *ingestion of the Other*.

'Cannibalism alone unites us. Socially. Economically. Philosophically...
The spirit refuses to conceive a language without a body. Need for the cannibalistic vaccine... against meridian religions. And against outside inquisitions... Cannibalism. The permanent transformation of the Taboo into a totem... Down with the vegetable elites. In communication with the soil.'[20]

The matter of the world is endlessly cooked and devoured. The stomach is the big outside us.

Before giving birth to modern chemistry, alchemy envisioned the whole universe as a boiling vat. If the fire of stars have been forever forging atoms, the inner cosmography of the human body deserves an *art of the living matter*.

Gastronomy must be rescued from the 'food design' imposed by the planetary petty bourgeoisie. The so-called 'molecular cuisine' reduced food to a mere sensorial fetishism (regulated by contrived physical parameters such as temperature, pressure and density) that neglects the basic cycle of *bios* within all edible matter.

The art of the living matter is the art to *remain true to the earth*,[21] not to its Origin but to its continuous generation – culinary materialism grows from the fertile ground of immanence, from the 'black earth' washed by the ancient Nile.[22]

The rise of modern medicine averted the same pagan ground. Witch-hunting was really the repression of women's autonomy and knowledge of nature's metabolism. *Domina herbarum* was the name given by the Inquisition to the 'witch of the fields'.

'Historically the witch was the village midwife, medic, soothsayer or sorceress... With the persecution of the folk healer, women were expropriated from a patrimony of empirical knowledge, regarding herbs and healing remedies, that they had accumulated and transmitted from generation to generation, its loss paving the way for a new form of enclosure. This was the rise of professional medicine, which erected in front of the 'lower classes' a wall of unchallengeable scientific knowledge, unaffordable and alien, despite its curative pretenses.'[23]

Breathing again the 'smell of the centuries'.

Any cook still wears the mask of death. Folklore like Cocaigne and Carnival remind us that the forgotten history of gastronomy is in fact the memory of deathly famines.[24] Recipes bear the overlooked cartography of empires at war, traces of migratory encounters and stratification of barbarian invasions.

Culinary art rose from the Dionysian inventiveness of the 'poor' against a hostile nature – never from a self-inflicted pauperism.

In contemporary times a new offspring of barbarians have reclaimed the city from within. The Unitary Urbanism advocated by the Situationists attempted to assault the 'urbanistic lie' and the separation of life into prisons of experience.[25]

Yet in Unitary Urbanism non-human forms of life were forgotten. Nature was not considered an autonomous force, let alone a potential ally. Situationism was playing within the utmost humanism: within the very tradition of the *human without substratum.*

Unlike Situationism, urban cannibalism is not a vagabond consumption. Instead of *détournement* urban cannibalism practices *dévournement* – a visceral occupation of the living city that does not merely chart its emotional geography.

In contemporary times other forces have also attempted to siege the city from within: sustainable development and its gardens emerged as the 'moral equivalent of war'. Nevertheless urban farming existed long before the upsurge of ecological correctness. Already in the Middle Ages allotments were inside defence walls to grow food during sieges.

And during WWII, as the Nazis were sinking the vessels bringing food to Britain, the campaign *Dig for Victory!* was a well-known national imperative. War allotments helped to save fuel and money for the troops, while Allied propaganda repeatedly bellowed: 'A victory garden is like a share in an airplane factory!'

Today the pacified horizon of sustainability appears like a wartime without war, the siege of a silent Ghost Army. The patriotic war *for* surplus has moved the home front to the inner front to become a war *on* surplus, through a highly individualized calculation of energy and water consumption, carbon footprint, intake of animal proteins and any culinary desire.

Within the ideology of de-growth we have alas established the borders of our own siege. Urban cannibals, eat the rich!

Limits to Growth: Taking Measures Can Still Avoid Collapse

Projections of the development of the world's population, resources, pollution, industrial output and food up till 2100 under two scenarios simulated by the World3 model. This model is based on the development of stocks like population, cultivated land, industrial capital and pollution. Left page: A scenario where no action is taken to prevent heavy impact on the environment caused by pollution and food shortage. Collapse

Population	Food	Resources	Industrial output	Pollution

starts around 2040. Right page: Technological advances limit industrial output, counter pollution, conserve resources and augment yields. Population growth is limited at 8 billion. A sustainable global society is born.

Source: D. Meadows, J. Randers and, D. Meadows, *Limits to growth: the 30-year update* (Vermont: Chelsea Green Publishing, 2004)

Population	Food	Resources	Industrial output	Pollution
900				
925				
950				
975				
000				
025				
050				
075				
100				

231

Waste and Recycling

238

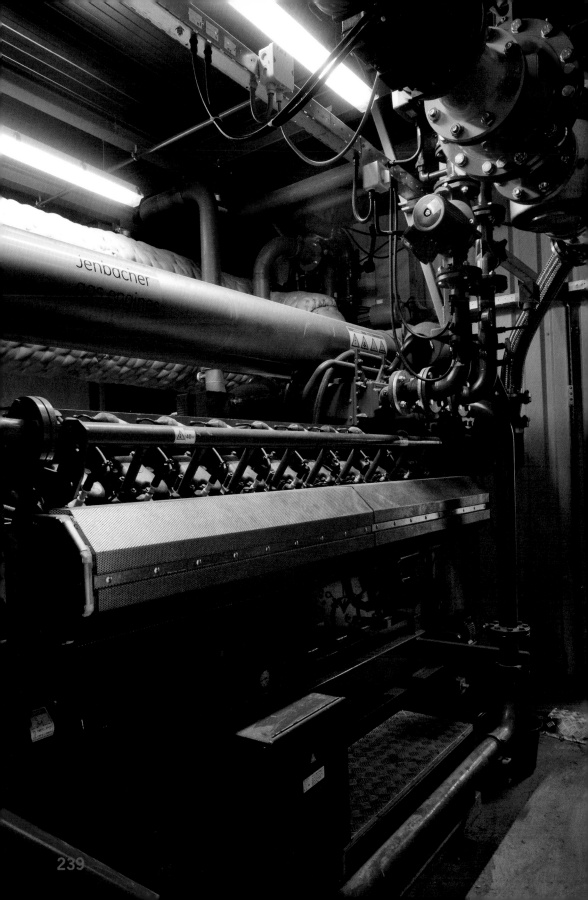

50cm

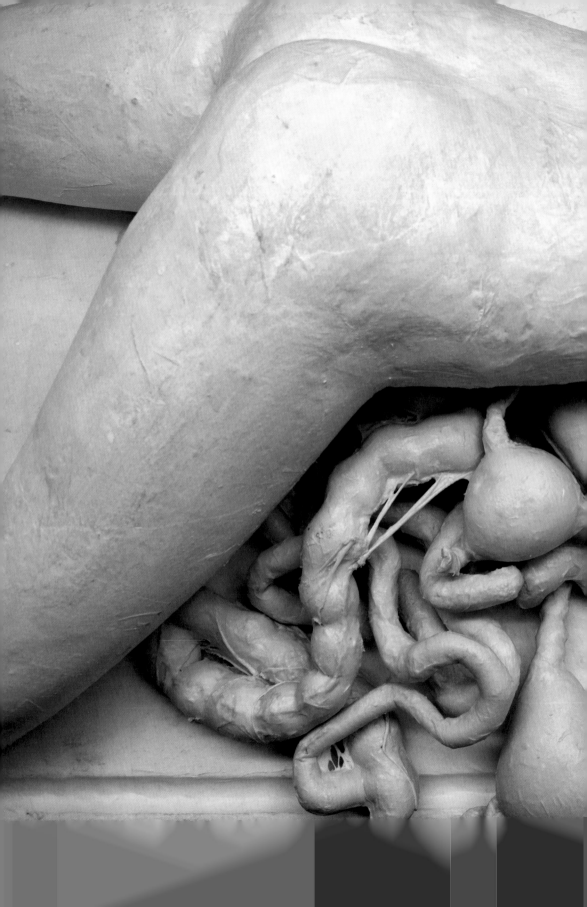

page 244

Freegans and dumpster divers employ alternative strategies for living, choosing limited participation in the conventional economy and minimal consumption of resources. As a protest against our society of consumerism and waste the movement is fairly new, but the idea of foraging for abandoned food of course is not; many people in the world have no other choice.

Photo: René Clement, 2007. Source: Hollandse Hoogte

page 245

A minority group of Coptic Christians recycle garbage in the impoverished Cairo neighbourhood Manshiayt Nasr, also known as El Mokattam or Garbage City. The 60,000 rubbish collectors, in Arabic *Zabaleen*, have been living this life for the past 70 to 80 years and have one of the highest recycle rates in the world: 80%. The award-winning 2009 documentary *Garbage Dreams* by filmmaker Mai Iskander gave the people an identity they seem proud of.

Photo: Teun Voeten, 2011. Source: Hollandse Hoogte

page. 246-247

Some call Atelier Van Lieshout's ecological design for recycling people cynical, but *Cradle to Cradle* of 2009 can at least be called radical. Young and healthy people can donate organs for transplantation, but those who are not so clever will be recycled in the meat-processing factory. Old, cripple and bad tasting people will end up in the biogas digester.

Photo and source: Atelier Van Lieshout

page 248

Nearly 2000 restaurants in San Francisco, California and thousands of single-family homes collect food scraps that are processed into high quality, nutrition rich compost and sold to farmers in the Bay Area. 20,000 tons of compost can be made out of every 100,000 tons of food scraps.

Photo: Justin Sullivan, 2009. Source: Getty Images

References
Timeline

A. Ullmann, 'Pasteur–Koch: Distinctive Ways of Thinking about Infectious Diseases: Linguistic misunderstandings along with genuine scientific differences over virulence and immunity drove the two geniuses apart', *Microbe Magazine* (2007) 2(8):383-387

Adams, Douglas, *The Hitchhiker's Guide to the Galaxy* (New York: Harmony Books, 1980)

'Appert, Nicholas.' New Standard Encyclopedia 1993 ed.

Atwood, M, *Oryx and Crake: A novel* (New York: Nan A. Talese, 2003)

Asimov, Isaac, *Foundation*, (Garden City, N.Y.: Doubleday, 1951)

Bailey, Gilbert E., *Vertical Farming*, (Baltimore: Lord Baltimore Press, 1915; digital edition)

Béarn, P, Grimod de la Reynière (Paris: Gallimard, 1930)

British Museum, www.britishmuseum.org; accessed in November 2011 http://www.britishmuseum.org/explore/highlights/highlight_objects/me/t/tablet,_allocation_of_beer.aspx.

Burroughs, E. R. *A Princess of Mars*. Reprint. (Charlottesville, Va: University of Virginia Library, 1993)

Carson, R., Darling, L., & Darling, L., *Silent Spring* (Boston: Houghton Mifflin, 1962)

Cato, M. P., Varro, M. T., Hooper, W. D., & In Ash, H. B., *On Agriculture*, (Cambridge, Mass: Harvard University Press, 1934)

Cayley, Arthur, the Younger, ed. *Memoirs of Sir Thomas More*, Vol II (London: Cadell and Davis, 1808)

Club of Rome. *The First Global Revolution* (1991). Publisher: Pantheon; 1st edition (September 3, 1991) as accessed on http://www.archive.org/details/TheFirstGlobalRevolution

Cohen, David (2011), 'Grow your own meat', BBC News, as accessed on 23 January 2012 at http://www.bbc.co.uk/news/technology-15402552

Collins, Nick (2011), 'First artificial burger to cost £250,000', *The Telegraph*, as accessed on 23 January 2012 at http://www.telegraph.co.uk/science/science-news/8733576/First-artificial-burger-to-cost-250000.html

Davies, R.W., *The Soviet Collective Farms, 1929-1930* (Macmillan, London, 1980)

Deutsch, Eliot. Dalvi, Rohit, *The Essential Vedanta* (Bloomington: World Wisdom, 2004; pg. 61)

Dick, Philip K., *Solar Lottery*, (New York: Vintage Books, 2003)

'Digging their way out of recession: Allotments by any other name', *The Economist* (2009), as accessed on 30 December 2011 at http://www.economist.com/node/13185476

Epstein, Ronald B., *Buddhist Text Translation Society's Buddhism A to Z*, (Burlingame, CA: Buddhist Text Translation Society, 2003)

Fairbairn, Brett, *The Meaning of Rochdale: The Rochdale Pioneers and the Co-operative Principles*, (Centre for the Study of Co-operatives, University of Saskatchewan, 1994)

FAO/WHO, *Understanding the Codex Alimentarius*, Third Edition. (Rome, issued by the Secretariat of the Joint FAO/WHO Food Standards Programme, 2006

G. Bruening and J.M. Lyons 'The case of the FLAVR SAVR tomato', *California Agriculture* (2000) 54(4):6-7

Gao, Mobo C. F., *The Battle for China's Past: Mao and the Cultural Revolution* (London: Pluto Press, 2008)

Greenberger, R., *The technology of ancient China* (New York: Rosen Pub. Group, 2006)

Grimod De La Reynière, *Encyclopedia of Food and Culture*, (Ed. Solomon H. Katz. Vol. 2. Gale Cengage, 1994)

Herbert, F., *Dune* (Philadelphia: Chilton Books, 1965)

Homer, Fagles, R., & Knox, B., *The Iliad* (New York, N.Y., U.S.A: Viking, 1990)

Hook and Norman, The Haskell F. Norman Library of Science and Medicine (1991) no. 59

Howard, E., Garden Cities of To-morrow, 2nd ed., (S. Sonnenschein & Co. Ltd., London, 1902)

Lasar, Matthew, 'Can we transport food like Internet data?' Foodtubes says yes, retrieved on 17 January 2012 at http://arstechnica.com/tech-policy/news/2010/12/want-fries-with-those-packets-introducing-foodtubes.ars

Lefebvre, H., *The production of space* (Oxford, OX, UK: Blackwell, 1991)

Levenstein, H. A., *Paradox of plenty: A social history of eating in modern America* (New York: Oxford University Press, 1993)

Lü, B., Knoblock, J. and Riegel, J. K., *The annals of Lü Buwei: a complete translation and study*, (Stanford, Calif: Stanford University Press, 2000)

Marx, Karl, *Capital Vol.3* (New York: Penguin, 1894/1991).

Ministry of Agriculture and Food, Norway, 'Svalbard Global Seed Vault', retrieved on 17 January 2012 at http://www.regjeringen.no/en/dep/lmd/campain/svalbard-global-seed-vault.html?id=462220

Mollison, Bill, *Permaculture: A Designers' Manual* (Tagari Publications, Australia, 1988)

Murph, Darren, 'The Cornucopia: MIT's 3D food printer patiently awaits 'the future', posted January 2010, retrieved on 17 January 2012 at http://www.engadget.com/2010/01/21/the-cornucopia-mits-3d-food-printer-patiently-awaits-the-futu/

Moore, Thomas, 2011, 'Dutch Scientist Plans £200k Lab Burger', Sky News, as accessed on 23 January 2012 at http://news.sky.com/home/strange-news/article/16110836

Patterson, T., 'Japan corners the market on square fruits.' June 15, 2001, CNN, as accessed in December 2011

Pohl, Frederik, and C. M. Kornbluth, *The Space Merchants* (New York: Walker, 1969)

Qur'àn. (2011). Retrieved December 30, 2011, from http://quran.com

Reade, J., *Mesopotamia* (Cambridge, Mass: Harvard University Press, 1991)

Reuters, 2011, 'First lab-grown burger coming right up ... that'll be $345,000', Reuters, as accessed on 23 January 2012 at http://www.msnbc.msn.com/id/45257771/ns/technology_and_science-science/t/first-lab-grown-burger-coming-right-thatll-be/#.Tx1K5WP-8tB

Reynolds, B. (2009), 'Feeding a World City: The London Food Strategy', *International Planning Studies*, 14:4, 417-424

Roosevelt, M. (2006) 'The Lure of the 100-Mile Diet', *Time Magazine*. Sunday June 11, 2006. Accessed on 19 January

2012 at http://www.time.com/time/maga-zine/article/0,9171,1200783,00.html

Saunders, C., US patent 1242872, 'Self-serving store', issued 1917-10-09
US patent 1242872, "Self-serving store", issued 1917-10-09
Schlosser, E., *Fast Food Nation: The Dark Side of the All-American Meal* (Boston: Houghton Mifflin, 2001)
Silverberg, R, *The Ends of Time* (Gillette, NJ: Cosmos Books, 2000)
Simak, C. D., *Time is the Simplest Thing* (Garden City, N.Y: Doubleday, 1961)
Sinclair, U., *The Jungle* (Cambridge, Mass: R. Bentley, 1971)
Soil Conservation and Domestic Allotment Act, Pub. L. No. 74-46, 49 Stat. 163 (1935), (Originally cited as ch. 85, 48 Stat. 31 (1935))
Specter, Michael, 2011, 'Test-Tube Burgers: How long will it be before you can eat meat that was made in a lab?', *The New Yorker*, as accessed on 23 January 2012 at http://www.newyorker.com reporting/2011/05/23/110523fa_fact_specter
Sterling, B., *Islands in the Net.* New York: Arbor House, p. 5, 19, 1988)

Temple, R. K. G., & Needham, J., *The Genius of China: 3,000 Years of Science, Discovery, and Invention* (New York: Simon and Schuster, 1986)
Tenn, W., *Immodest Proposals: The Complete Science Fiction of William Tenn* (Framingham, MA: NESFA Press, 2001)
Thoreau, H. D., *Walden, or, Life in the Woods; and On the Duty of Civil Disobedience* (New York: New American Library, 1963)
Toussaint-Samat, M. and Blackwell, E.B.L. *A history of Food*, (Chichester, West Sussex, U.K: Wiley-Blackwell, 2009)

Walsh, B., 'The Planet's Ultimate Backup Plan': Svalbard', *Time Magazine* (27 February 2009), retrieved 17 January 17, 2012.
Webster, George, 'Farm in the city could be supermarket of the future', CNN, October 29, 2011; retrieved on 17 January 2012 at http://edition.cnn.com/2011/10/29/world/europe/holland-park-supermarket/index.html
Wessels Living History Farm (2003), 'Hybrid Crops', as accessed on Nov. 2011 at Web site http://www.living-historyfarm.org.
Wright, Frank Lloyd, *The Disappearing City* (New York, W. F. Payson, 1932)

'Where It Began . . .', *PigglyWiggly.com*. Piggly Wiggly LLC. As accessed on 21 November 2008

Zaehner, R. C., *The Bhagavad-Gītā* (London: Oxford University Press, 1973)

Notes

Foodprint: Artistic Reflections on Practical Issues

1 With thanks to Maaike Lauwaert, Francien van Westrenen, and Arno van Roosmalen. A modified version of this text is included in the Valiz publication *Nils Norman Eetbaar Park/Edible Park*, that will appear simultaneously.

2 For instance artists such as Joep van Lieshout, Rirkrit Tiravanija, Ollivier Darné, Fritz Haeg, Raul Ortega Ayala, Zeger Reyers, Debra Solomon, and John Bock; designers such as Dunne & Raby, Ton Matton, and Christien Meindertsma; and architects such as Aldo Cibic, Bohn & Viljoen, or Winy Maas.

3 This project was jointly commissioned by Stroom Den Haag, InnovationNetwork and the Pig Farming section of LTO (the Dutch Federation of Agriculture and Horticulture).

4 Commissioned by Stroom and the Province of South Holland, in partnership with Alterra Wageningen.

5 Both projects were still running as this book went to press.

6 Norman and Stroom Den Haag collaborated on this project with the Municipality of The Hague, the amateur gardeners' association Nut en Genoegen, and a local group of permaculturists.

7 Solomon has her own foundation, 'URBANIAHOEVE, social design lab for urban agriculture', and is realizing the project together with residents, schools, the city of The Hague, a housing corporation, and various community organizations.

8 Sandra Spijkerman, 'Foodprint: voedsel voor de stad, voer voor de kunst', *Kunstbeeld* 12/1, 2011-2012, p. 81.

Permaculture as a Permanent Culture

1 Angelo documents his strategies and his harvests at www.deepgreenpermaculture. com.

2 Paddy Manning, 'Peak oil: it's closer than you think', *Sydney Morning Herald*, April 30, 2011, http://www.smh.com.au/business/peak-oil-its-closer-than-you-think-20110429-1e0gt.html.

3 Chriss Vernon, 'Coal - The Roundup', *The Oil Drum: Europe*, July 12, 2007, http://europe.theoildrum.com/node/2726/.

4 Adam Grubb, 'Peak oil primer', *Energy Bulletin*, April 13, 2003, (October 20, 2011 update), http://www.energybulletin.net/primer.

5 R. Heinberg, *Powerdown: Options and Actions for a Post-carbon World* (New Society Publishers, 2004).

6 Holmgren, 'What is Sustainability?', in *Collected Writings & Presentations 1978-2006* (Holmgren Design Services, 2003), permacultureprinciples.com/downloads/33_what_is_sustainability.pdf.

7 D. Holmgren, *Permaculture: Principles & Pathways Beyond Sustainability* (Holmgren Design Services, 2002).

8 T. Hemenway, *Gaia's Garden: A Guide to Home-Scale Permaculture* (Chelsea Green Publishing, 2009).

9 The influence of permaculturists in Cuba is partially documented in the film *The Power of Community, How Cuba Survived Peak Oil* (2006).

10 Sinan Koont, 'The Urban Agriculture of Havana', Monthly Review, January 2009, http://monthlyreview.org/2009/01/01/the-urban-agriculture-of-havana.

11 Natasha Mitchell, 'Nature Deficit Disorder: the mind in urban combat', *All In The Mind* (Radio National (Australian Broadcasting Corporation), April 17, 2010).

12 Marc G Berman, John Jonides, and Stephen Kaplan, 'The Cognitive Benefits of Interacting With Nature', *Psychological Science* 19, no. 12 (2008): 1207-1212.

13 George Monbiot, 'Feeding Crime', *Monbiot.com*, June 2, 2006, http://www.monbiot.com/2006/05/02/feeding-crime/.

14 D. E. Barrett and M. Radke-Yarrow, 'Effects of nutritional supplementation on children's responses to novel, frustrating, and competitive situations', *The American Journal of Clinical Nutrition* 42, no. 1 (1985): 102-120.

Feeding the World: A New Paradigm for 2050

1 For example, India alone accounts for 37% of the 535 million children that between the ages of six months and five years suffer from moderate to severe vitamin A deficiency.

Solving the Problems of Food Production in 2050 through Synthetic Genomics Technology

1 Synthetic Genomics Inc., 11149 N. Torrey Pines Road, La Jolla, CA 92037.

2 The J. Craig Venter Institute, 10355 Science Center Drive, San Diego, CA 92121.

3 Synthetic Genomics Inc., 11149 N. Torrey Pines Road, La Jolla, CA 92037.

4 Food and Agriculture Organization United Nations, *How to Feed the World in 2050* (FAO, 2009).

5 World Health Organization, Food and Agriculture Organization, *Diet, Nutrition and the Prevention of Chronic Diseases* (United Nations, 2003).

6 J. Sheeran, The Challenges of Food Security: Report from the Barilla Center for Food & Nutrition (Barilla Center for Food & Nutrition, 2009).

7 E. Millstone, & T. Lang, *The Atlas of Food: Who Eats What, Where and Why* (Berkeley: University of California Press, 2008).

8 Food and Agriculture Organization United Nations, *Global Capture and Aquaculture Production* (FAO, 2010).
IFFO, *Global Production of Fishmeal & Fish Oil* (IFFO, 2008).
Indexmundi, *Historical Fishmeal Prices* (Indexmundi, 2010).

9 P. Dery, & B. Anderson, (2007). 'Peak Phosphorus', *Energy Bulletin*, (2007), 1-16. A. Fry, & E. Haden, Facts and Trends: Water, Report of the World Business Council for Sustainable Development (World Business Council for Sustainable Development, 2006).

10 J. Sheeran, The Challenges of Food Security: Report from the Barilla Center for Food & Nutrition (Barilla Center for Food & Nutrition, 2009).

11 M, Wiebe, 'Quorn Myco-protein – Overview of a Successful Fungal Product', *Mycologist* (2004), 18(1), 17-20.

12 M.R. Edwards, Freedom Foods: Superior New Foods, low on the Food Chain for People, Producers and Our Planet (Seattle: CreateSpace, 2011).

13 L. Lai, J.X. Kang, R. Li, J. Wang, W.T. Witt, H.Y. Yong, et al., 'Generation of Cloned Transgenic Pigs Rich in Omega-3 Fatty Acids'. *Nature Biotechnology* (2006), 24(4), 435-436.

14 E. Marris, 'Transgenic Fish Go Large', *Scientific American* (2010, September 14), 14.

15 D.G. Gibson, J. I. Glass, C. Latigue, V. N. Noskov, R.-Y. Chuang, M. A. Algire, et al., 'Creation of a Bacterial Cell Controlled by a Chemically Synthesized Genome', *Science* (2010), 329, 52-56.

16 The White House, *The Ethics of Synthetic Biology and Emerging Technologies* (Presidential Commission for the Study of Bioethical Issues, 2010).

Arctic Food Network

1 S. Meakin, T. Kurvits, *Assessing The Impacts of Climate Change On Food Security*

In The Canadian Arctic. Prepared by GRID-Arendal for Indian and Northern Affairs Canada (March 2009) http://www.grida.no/files/publications/foodsec_updt_LA_lo.pdf (accessed 2 February 2012).

2   Ibid.

3   J. D. Ford, M. Beaumier, 'Feeding the family during times of stress: experience and determinants of food insecurity in an Inuit community,"The Geographical Journal (July 2010) vol. 177, no. 1.

Women's Quest to Secure Food in Post-Conflict East Africa

1   M. Kimani, 'Women struggle to Secure Land Rights', Africa Renewal (April 2008), Vol.22 #1, 10.

2   I. Rose, 'Women's Land Access in Post-Conflict Rwanda: Bridging the Gap between Customary Land Law and Pending Land Legislation', Texas Journal of Women and Law (13 February 2004), 197-250.

3   M. Mwagiru, Women's Land and Property Rights in Three Eastern Africa Countries. Women's Land and Property Rights in Situations of Conflict and Reconstruction. A Reader based on the February, 1998 Inter-Regional Consultation in Kigali, Rwanda (New York: United Nations Development Fund for Women [UNIFEM], 2001), 18-23.

4   S. Pantuliano, 'The Land Question: Sudan's Peace nemesis', Humanitarian Policy Group Working Paper (December 2007).

5   I. Rose, 'Women's Land Access in Post-Conflict Rwanda', op. cit. (note 2).

6   G. G. Paradza, 'Securing women's land rights in Eastern Africa: Time for a paradigm shift', International Land Coalition Policy Brief (March 2011), no. 3.

7   Rwanda Women's Network, Experiences of Women Asserting their Land Rights. The Case of Bugesera District (Rome: SWAL Research Report. International Land Coalition, 2011).

8   G. G. Paradza,' Innovations for Securing Women's Access to Land in East Africa', International Land Coalition Working Paper (2011), no. 13.

9   Rwanda Women's Network, Experiences of Women Asserting their Land Rights, op. cit. (note7).

10   Joint Assessment Mission of the Governments of Belgium, Canada, Netherlands, Norway, Sweden and the United Kingdom with the Ministry of Gender and Women in Development, Ministry of Local Government, Beijing Secretariat, ProFemme/Twese Hamwe and the Women's Counsils and

UNDP and UNIFEM, Report of the Learning Oriented Assessment of Gender Main-streaming and Women Empowerment Strate-gies in Rwanda (Kigali: September 2002).

11   G. G. Paradza, 'Securing women's land rights in Eastern Africa', op. cit. (note 6).

12   Ibid.

13   Joint Assessment Mission, Report, op. cit. (note 10).

14   G. G. Paradza, 'Innovations for Securing Women's Access to Land in East Africa', op. cit. (note 8).

Manifesto of Urban Cannibalism

(Amsterdam Declaration)

1   K. Marx, Grundrisse (1858).

2   G. Deleuze, F. Guattari, Mille Plateaux (Paris: Minuit, 1980).

3   F. Braudel, Civilisation matérielle, économie et capitalisme (Paris: Armand Colin, 1967).

4   M.Kaika, City of Flows: Modernity, Nature, and the City (New York : Routledge, 2004).

5   M. Delanda, A Thousand Years of Nonlinear History (New York: Zone Books, 1997).

6   J. Moore (2010), 'Amsterdam is Standing on Norway', Online. Available http://www.jasonwmoore.com/Essays.html (accessed 15 February 2012).

7   M. Foucault, Surveiller et punir (Paris: Gallimard, 1975).

8   G. Clement, Manifeste pour le Tier-paysage (Paris: Éditions Sujet/Objet, 2004).

9   O. De Andrade, 'Manifesto Antropófago', Revista de Antropofagia (São Paulo), no.1 (May 1928): 3-7.

10   As in: B. Latour, Nous n'avons jamais été modernes: Essai d'anthropologie symétrique (Paris: La Découverte, 1991).

11   M. Serres, Le Parasite (Paris: Grasset, 1980).

12   Ibid.

13   F. Jullien, Nourrir sa vie: A l'écart du Bonheur (Paris: Seuil, 2005).

14   L. Margulis, Origin of Eukaryotic Cells (New Haven-London: Yale University Press, 1970).

15   Novalis, Teplitz Fragments (1798).

16   B. Spinoza, Ethica (1677).

17   The Latin word sapiens derives from sapor, that means 'taste'.

18   G. Deleuze and Felix Guattari, L'Anti-Œdipe (Paris: Minuit, 1972).

19   D. Birnbaum, A. Olsson(2009), An Interview with Jacques Derrida on the Limits of Digestion, Online. Available http://

www.e-flux.com/journal/an-interview-with-jacques-derrida-on-the-limits-of-digestion/ (accessed 15 February 2012).

20   O. De Andrade, Manifesto Antropófago, op. cit. (note 9).

21   F. Nietzsche, Also sprach Zarathustra (1883).

22   The most recognized etymology of 'alchemy' is the Ancient Egyptian word keme, or 'black earth', which was another name for Egypt, as a fertile dark soil opposed to the dry light sand of the desert.

23   S. Federici, Caliban and the Witch: Women, The Body, and Primitive Accumulation (New York: Autonomedia, 2004).

24   P. Camporesi, Il paese della fame (Bologna: Il mulino, 1978).

25   A. Kotányi and R. Vaneigem, 'Programme elementaire du Bureau d'urbanisme unitaire', Internationale Situationniste, no. 6 (Paris: August, 1961).

Credits

This publication has been made possible with the financial support of the DOEN Foundation, Mondriaan Fund and the Netherlands Architecture Fund.

This publication is part of the Foodprint programme at art and architecture centre Stroom Den Haag.

Editor in chief/concept
Brigitte van der Sande

Editorial board
**Maaike Lauwaert,
Peter de Rooden,
Francien van Westrenen
(Stroom Den Haag)**

Image editors
Beukers Scholma, Brigitte van der Sande, Minouche Wardenaar

Timeline editor
Amanda Berne

Infographics editor
Gilles Havik

Copy editor
Leo Reijnen

Copyright editor
Dyveke Rood

Dutch-English translation
Bookmakers, Nijmegen

Portuguese-English translation
Bookmakers, Nijmegen

Graphic design
Beukers Scholma, Haarlem

Printing and lithography
Die Keure, Bruges

Publisher
Marcel Witvoet, NAi Publishers

Printed and bound in
Belgium

ISBN
978-90-5662-854-3

We would like to thank all the contributing authors, as well as:
**Jacques Abelman
Atelier van Lieshout
Van Bergen Kolpa Architecten
Carlijn Bouten (TUE)
Floris van Breugel
CIMMYT (Dave Hoisington)
Agnes Denes
Agnes Dherbeys
Anthony Dunne and Fiona Raby
Jack Dykinga
Maarten Vanden Eynde
Food and Agriculture Organization
of the United Nations (photography
Walter Astrada, Giuseppe Bizzarri,
Saeed Khan, Ishara Kodikara,
Farooq Naeem, Giulio Napolitano,
Sophia Paris, Ami Vitale, H. Wagner)
GRO Holland
Adam Grubb
Charles Haynes
Arne Hendriks
ILRI (Steve Mann)
James King
The International Institute of Tropical
Agriculture in Nigeria (IITA)
Izvora
Christian Jankowski
Karin Kaldenhoven
Lateral Office
Winy Maas/The Why Factory
NASA
Marie-Lan Nguyen
Michiko Nitta and Michael Burton
John O'Shea
PlantLab
Philips Design
Ferdinand Reus
Rijksmuseum van Oudheden, Leiden
Nick Saltmarsh
Allan Sekula and Noël Burch
Min Shin and James Little
Debra Solomon
Mari Tefre/Svalbard Global Seed Vault
Wageningen University and Research
Harvey Wang
Yvonne Wassink
Fotoflug Wildeshausen**

Mondriaan Stichting
(Mondriaan Foundation)

Stimuleringsfonds voor Architectuur

the Netherlands Architecture Fund

FSC
www.fsc.org
MIX
Papier van verantwoorde herkomst
FSC® C009115

© 2012 The authors, Stroom Den Haag
and NAi Publishers, Rotterdam
All rights reserved. No part of this publication
may be reproduced, stored in a retrieval
system, or transmitted in any form or by
any means, electronic, mechanical, photo-
copying, recording or otherwise, without the
prior written permission of the publisher.

For works of visual artists affiliated with
a CISAC-organization the copyrights have
been settled with Pictoright in Amsterdam.
© 2012, c/o Pictoright Amsterdam

Although every effort was made to find
the copyright holders for the illustrations
used, it has not been possible to trace
them all. Interested parties are requested
to contact NAi Publishers, Mauritsweg 23,
3012 JR Rotterdam, The Netherlands.

**NAi Publishers is an internationally
orientated publisher specialized in
developing, producing and distributing
books on architecture, visual arts and
related disciplines.**
www.naipublishers.nl

**Available in North, South and Central
America through D.A.P./Distributed Art
Publishers Inc**
155 Sixth Avenue 2nd Floor
New York
NY 10013-1507
tel +1 212 627 1999
fax +1 212 627 9484
dap@dapinc.com

**Available in the United Kingdom and
Ireland through Art Data**
12 Bell Industrial Estate
50 Cunnington Street
London W4 5HB
tel +44 208 747 1061
fax +44 208 742 2319
orders@artdata.co.uk

'boond boond se sagar banta hai'

every drop contributes to the making of the ocean